Show Time!

Show Time!

Music, Dance, and Drama
Activities for Kids

Lisa Bany-Winters

CHICAGO
REVIEW
PRESS

Library of Congress Cataloging-in-Publication Data

Bany-Winters, Lisa
    Show time! : music, dance, and drama activities for kids / Lisa Bany-Winters.
        p. cm.
    Includes bibliographical references.
    Summary: Introduces the concepts of music, dance, and acting, suggesting how to
create a musical production through games and role-playing and describing all aspects of
a show from auditions to curtain call.
    ISBN 1-55652-361-0
    1. Musicals—Juvenile—Production and direction—Juvenile literature. 2.
Musicals—History and criticism—Juvenile literature. [1. Musicals—Production and
direction.] I. Title.

MT955 .B218 2000
782.6'0232'083—dc21
                                                              99-045339

Cover and interior illustrations and design: © 2000 Fran Lee

The author and the publisher disclaim all liability for
use of the information contained in this book.

Published by Chicago Review Press, Incorporated
814 North Franklin Street
Chicago, Illinois 60610
ISBN 978-1-55652-361-8
Printed in the United States of America
10 9 8 7 6

For Michaela

and everyone who will play with her

Contents

3

4

5

6

Acknowledgments

g'd like to thank Stephanie and Joe Albright, Nancy and John Bany, Martin Bany, Carley and Vincent Brackett, Ginni Brackett, Fran Brumlik, Hylin Burrows, Alison and Erica Cherry, Geoff Coates, Martin de Maat, Ann Elyachar, the Emanon Theater Company, the Evanston Arts Camp, Everybody Move, Inc., Leslie Felbain, Larrance Fingerhut, Richard Friedman, Dan Gold, Larry Grimm, Gymboree, Laura Holliday, Amy Harmon, Kristie Hassinger, the Highland Park Arts Camp, Ashley Hugen, the Illinois Theater Association, Margaret James, B.J. Jones, Barbara Kanady, Ruth Kane, Hope Kaye, Marcy Konlon, K.D. Kweskin, Karen LaShelle, Sarah Levine, Susie Lindenbaum, Jason Long, Jason Lubow, Laura Maloney, Nora McCready, Kristie McGonagle, Anthony McKinney, Ed Nishioka, the Northlight Kids Improv Class, the Northlight Theatre, the Old Town School of Folk Music, Ron Packowitz, Sheldon Patinkin, Jerry Proffit, Danny Robles, Lisa Rosenthal, Peter Rybolt, Dr. Seuss, Cynthia Sherry, Cheryl Sloane, TeenStreet Theatre, Klahr Thorsen, Chas Vrba, K. Michelle Walker, Katrina Wandel, Janie Weisenberg, Wiggle Worms, Brian Winters, and Devorah Zion.

I'd like to thank the original cast for the plays listed in Chapter 8. The cast for *Paul Bunyan, Davy Crockett*, and *Sluefoot Sue* included Joe Albright as Paul, cow, book learning folk, and a coyote; Chas Vrba as the King of Sweden, Creampuff Fatty, Davy, Pa, and a coyote; Barbara Kanady as Tim Ber, book learning folk, Ma, and a coyote; Marcy Konlon as Sourdough Slim, the Panther, and Sue. The cast for *The Three Little Pigs, Goldilocks and The Three Bears*, and *The Three Billy Goats Gruff* included Janet Tuegel as the Wolf, Mama Bear, and the Troll; Kerri Smith as Pig 3, Papa Bear, and the Little Billy Goat; Joe Albright as Pig 2, Goldilocks, and the Big Billy Goat; and Rachel Pergl as Pig 1, Baby Bear, and the Middle Billy Goat. The cast for *Alice in Wonderland* included Stephanie Albright as Alice; Joe Albright as the White Rabbit; Klahr Thorsen as The Queen of Hearts; Brian Winters as the Mad Hatter; Anthony McKinney as the March Hare, Geoff Coates as the Duchess and the Doormouse, Danny Robles as the Cook and the Caterpillar, Ed Nishioka and Jason Lubow as the Cheshire Cat.

Introduction

Musicals are often our first introduction to the theater. *Annie, The Wizard of Oz, Beauty and the Beast,* and other family musicals are the first plays many young people see. Dance classes often start at age three, and children begin to sing almost as soon as they can talk.

Everyone who enjoys singing, dancing, acting, or watching musical theater will enjoy the games and activities in this book.

A performer who can sing, dance, and act is sometimes called a *triple threat*. In this book you will find a triple threat of activities. Music, dance, and drama are all part of musical theater. They provide three times the fun whether you are a fan, a game player, or an aspiring triple threat.

Teachers, directors, and choreographers use games and activities to prepare performers for their shows. Games are a fun way to practice performance skills and develop self-confidence. Parents can play many of these games with their children while at home, in the car, waiting in a doctor's office, and any other time you have a few minutes to spare. Singing, dancing, and acting are wonderful things for a family to do together. You can even create your own family songs, poems, or shows to perform at holidays and other gatherings.

"The History of Musical Theater" overviews where theater's

been and shows how far it's come. It also lists important musical theater terms, identifies who does what job, and what everything means. Here you'll not only find information on the history of musicals, but also musicals about history, such as *1776*.

"Musical Themes" divides musicals by their themes or topics. If you have a favorite musical, or will be performing in one, you'll find games and activities here that may fit the theme of your musical and enhance your enjoyment of the performance.

"Musical Reviews" features ideas and activities for creating musical variety shows. A review is a show put together with a combination of songs, scenes, skits, and/or dance, often tied to a theme. If you'd like to create your own review, you'll find activities here for creating original stories and characters as well as ideas for themes.

"A Performer Prepares" takes you through an actor's performance in a play, beginning with auditions, through vocal warm-ups, to how to write your biography for the program, and ending with how to take a bow and receive applause at the end of your performance. With fun games and exercises, you'll learn how actors memorize their lines and what they do to prepare for a role.

If you play a musical instrument or sing, you will find the

games and activities in "I Got Rhythm" helpful and fun. Rhythm, songwriting, and even breath-support are a few of the skills that can be learned with these musical games.

If you like to move you'll feel like dancing when you see all of the fun games in "Gotta Dance." Whether you are a skilled dancer or just love to dance around your living room, these activities will give you ideas for creative moves.

Theater games, such as those found in "An Actor's Life for Me" are great for parties, rehearsals, and other indoor and outdoor fun. Directors and teachers have used theater games for years to help actors learn to work together, focus, develop their characters, and boost their energy at rehearsal.

If it's scripts you're looking for, you'll find a variety of short plays and scenes for young people in "Show Time!" From folk tales, such as *Paul Bunyan,* to classics, such as *Alice in Wonderland*, these scripts are sure to get your creative juices flowing.

Viola Spolin, author of *Improvisation for the Theater*, *Theater Games for Rehearsal*, and *Theater Games for the Classroom*, first introduced the idea of teaching theater through games. Actors have been using games ever since. Games are a fun way to expand your creativity, sharpen your focus, learn to work with others on projects, and build self-confidence. These games are for everyone, not just those serious about becoming actors. So put on your dancing shoes and get ready to play, because it's *Show Time!*

The History of Musical Theater

William Shakespeare filled his comedies with music. In *A Midsummer Night's Dream*, the fairies sing and dance for their fairy queen. French playwright Molière also included songs in his plays. In *A Doctor in Spite of Himself*, the doctor prescribes "a song with a merry note, and a dance with a lively step" to cure some of his patients. Later Molière worked with composer Jean-Baptiste Lully to create comedy-ballets. These were some of the first known dramas that included music and dance, although they were not quite what we would call musicals today.

Musicals came about as composers began to parody or poke fun at opera. They lightened the mood of the music and changed its style to be similar to popular music of the day. *The Pirates of Penzance*, which hit Broadway in 1879, was one of the first musicals.

In the 1920s, Tin Pan Alley, a district of composers and publishers of popular music in New York City, was the hot spot for American musicals. Many songwriters, including Irving Berlin and George Gershwin, created musicals in these publishing houses.

In 1927 musicals began to take on all sorts of themes, both comedic and serious. *Show Boat* was the first musical that had songs that actually moved the plot forward, a breakthrough for telling stories in musical theater style.

The term *musical* was shortened from the term "musical comedy," but it now refers to dramas as well as comedies.

In 1960 the first rock-and-roll musical hit the stage. It was called *Bye Bye Birdie*, and told a story similar to what happened when Elvis Presley was drafted. It also includes a grown-up love story that follows the standard "boy gets girl, boy loses girl, boy gets girl" back plot of earlier musical comedies. Many rock musicals have since followed.

Today Andrew Lloyd Webber and others continue to add to the wealth of musical theater. Many actors say that live musical theater is where they began, and it is still their favorite venue. Musicals continue to be a favorite among theatergoers, especially young people.

Chorus Game

In ancient Greece and even in Shakespeare's time, the *chorus* was *not* a group of people who sing songs together in a play as we use the term today. Instead, the chorus was one actor who often told the audience what was about to happen in that scene. This was because there were few surprise endings in early theater. Playwrights wanted the audience to know the story before they watched the performance. Since they didn't show very much violence on stage at that time either, the chorus would also tell the audience if someone was hurt. Another job of the chorus was to announce the passing of time, so the audience would know if the next scene happened years or only moments after the previous scene.

This is an improvisation game that shows the job of the chorus before the invention of musical theater. *Improvisation* (also known as *improv*) is a style of acting where you create, without any advance preparation. Here the chorus tells the story before the other players act it out; but, because this is improv, the players don't know in advance what the chorus will say.

Choose one player to be the chorus. The other players will be actors. The chorus steps out and says what will happen in the first of three scenes. Because you are improvising and not using a script, the chorus makes up what will happen. The actors have to listen carefully. After the chorus finishes explaining the scene, the actors act it out. The chorus then explains scene two, and the actors act it out. Next, the chorus explains scene three, and the actors act it out.

This exercise can be used for playwriting and other creative writing because it teaches the concept of beginning, middle, and end, and lets you see the story you are making up.

Here is an example of how this game might go.

Stephanie is the chorus. Joe and Charlie are the actors improvising the scenes. Here is an example of what they all might say.

• •

STEPHANIE

Ladies and gentlemen, this is the story of a duck and a bunny. The duck is very sad and lonely. He has lost his quack. His bunny friend hops all over trying to find it.

JOE

(becomes the duck)

I'm so sad. I've lost my quack. Listen.

(HE tries to quack, but nothing comes out.)

See?

(HE cries.)

CHARLIE

(acting as the bunny)

Don't be sad, my duck friend. I'll find your quack.

(HE hops around while saying)

Has anyone seen a quack? No? Oh, where can it be?

(HE exits.)

STEPHANIE

In scene two the bunny comes back to the duck. He has found all sorts of sounds, but none of them is a quack.

CHARLIE

Duck! Duck! I think I've found what you're looking for. Here it is.

(opening his mouth wide)

Mooooo!

JOE

That's not my quack. That's a moo. That belongs to Mrs. Cow.

CHARLIE

Oh. Well, don't worry. I think I've got it. Is this it?

(opening his mouth wide)

Oink!

JOE

No! That's not my quack either! That belongs to Mr. Pig.

CHARLIE

I've got one more. This has got to be it.

(opening his mouth wide)

Baaaaa!

JOE

That's not it either! That's Señor Sheep's! We'll never find my quack.

STEPHANIE

The bunny went off searching again, determined to find the duck's quack. While he was gone, the duck heard something coming from a raspberry bush. A raspberry was saying "quack." He ate the raspberry and got his quack back. When the bunny returned, exhausted, the duck made him a raspberry pie.

JOE

I hope Bunny finds my quack soon. Wait, I think I hear something. That bush is quacking! It's not the bush, it's this little raspberry.

(HE eats the raspberry.)

That was tasty.

(opening his mouth wide)

Quack! It's my quack!

(opening his mouth wide again)

Quack! I've got it back!

CHARLIE

(entering)

Well Duck, I've looked everywhere, but I could not find your quack.

JOE

(opening his mouth wide)

Quack!

CHARLIE

You've got it! Where did you find it?

Quack!

JOE

It was in a raspberry. I ate the raspberry and it came back.

CHARLIE

To think I looked all over the forest and it was right here. Speaking of raspberries, I sure am hungry after all that looking.

JOE

You're such a great friend. I'm going to make you a raspberry pie.

STEPHANIE

Curtain

In ballet a group of dancers who dance together is called the *corps de ballet*.

Musical Theater Terms

Here are some commonly used theater terms and their definitions.

Act A long part of a play made up of scenes. Most musicals have two acts, referred to as "Act I" and "Act II," with an intermission (see definition) in the middle.

Actor Anyone who acts. Can apply to both male and female performers.

Audition Tryouts for a play. The director usually watches a short performance, such as a monologue (see definition), dance, or song, in order to select actors to play each role.

Ballad A song that tells a story or a sentimental song sung at a slow tempo.

Bio Short for biography, a paragraph about each actor and staff member who is part of a play's production. Bios appear in the program.

Blocking Charting out the movement of stage performers. Indicating where each actor stands and moves onstage throughout a play.

Broadway The New York City theater district.

Callback A second audition. After the initial auditions the director may narrow down a smaller group of actors she wants to see again. The callback audition helps the director make her final decisions.

Cancan A French dance that usually involves lines of high-kicking dancers; often used in musical theater.

Choreographer The person who stages and blocks (see definition for blocking) dances.

Chorus A group of people who sing or dance in a musical, but have few lines to say. This is the modern definition of this term. (See **Chorus Game** for the original definition of the chorus term.)

Dance captain A staff person (often from the dance chorus) who is in charge of rehearsing the dances after the choreographer has staged and blocked them.

Director The person who stages all the movement onstage (other than dance), develops the concept for the play, and casts the play.

Duet A song for two singers.

Encore A song at the end of a show done because the audience has applauded so much that the performers would like to perform for them one more time.

Intermission A break in the play between acts, giving the audience a chance to stretch or get refreshments, and the stage crew a chance to change the sets.

Jazz dance A style of dance that involves moving hands and legs independently, with the pelvis as the center of movement. Keeping the hands wide and walking low and with wide steps are some of the movements characteristic of jazz dance.

Libretto   A musical script that includes lyrics.

Modern dance   A style of dance using free movements and dramatic expression.

Monologue   A speech given by one character in a play. Often used in auditions by actors.

Musical   Originally short for musical comedy, but now refers to all musicals, whether they are comedies or dramas.

Musical Director   The person in charge of the music elements of a musical, including directing the actors in their songs and working with the orchestra.

Off Broadway   A theater located in New York City, but not in the Broadway theater district, and having less than 300 seats.

Operetta   Meaning little opera. It's usually lighter than an opera and includes some talking.

Score   Sheet music showing the singing and instrument parts of a play.

Opening Night   The first night of a play's production run. Sometimes called press night because this is the night the press is invited to see the play and review it for the newspapers.

Preview   Performances before opening night, usually sold to the audience at a lower cost than tickets during regular-run performances. These performances give the director a chance to see the audience's response to a play and to make changes or adjustments if needed before the press opening. When George Gershwin's musical *Porgy and Bess* first previewed on Broadway, it ran for four hours. It was shortened by about an hour before opening night.

Showstopper   A big production number in a play that is popular with the audience. The name comes from the audience applauding for so long that the show has to be stopped until the applause dies down.

Syncopation   A rhythm that emphasizes the off beat. The rhythm is shifted so that the beat that is normally softer is stressed and the beat that is normally stressed is weak.

Tap dance   A dance performed with taps on the dancers' shoes.

Understudy   An actor who learns one or more parts in a play and is ready to perform in case another actor gets sick or is unable to perform.

West End   The London theater district.

There are theater angels! *Angel* is the term given to a person who financially backs a play.

Direction Game

The job of the *director* is most easily done when the actors listen and pay close attention to her. She tells them where to go onstage and helps them decide how to say their lines. This game helps actors get used to listening and following directions. Players can give directions to one another and see what happens when everyone falls, walks, or freezes at the same time.

 Begin with a short list of standard directions. Here are some ideas.

- ✦ Fall
- ✦ Freeze
- ✦ Run
- ✦ Sit
- ✦ Walk
- ✦ Turn

Begin with all players walking around the room. At any time, one player calls out a direction. As soon as the player calls out the action, all of the players (including the one who called it out) follow that direction until another direction is called. Try to work together so that only one direction is called out at a time. Here's an example.

Caroline, Julie, Amy, Josh, and Dante are walking around.

JOSH

Freeze!
(Everyone freezes. Everyone stays frozen until CAROLINE speaks.)

CAROLINE

Walk!
(Everyone walks. Everyone continues to walk until JULIE speaks.)

JULIE

Fall!
(Everyone falls and stays on the ground until DANTE speaks.)

DANTE

Run!
(Everyone gets up and runs until AMY speaks.)

AMY

Sit!
(Everyone sits.)

After you have played with just five predetermined directions, try playing the game with any directions you can think of. Listen carefully because the players can call out anything they like. Here are some ideas.

- ◆ Clap
- ◆ Climb
- ◆ Crawl
- ◆ Cry
- ◆ Dance

- ◆ Hop
- ◆ Kick
- ◆ Lean
- ◆ Roll over
- ◆ Sleep

- ◆ Sneeze
- ◆ Squat
- ◆ Stomp
- ◆ Twist
- ◆ Yell

Arabesque is a dance move where the dancer lifts one outstretched leg behind her to make a shape.

Historical Musicals

*E*vita and *1776* are musicals based on actual events in history. *1776* tells the story of the American Revolution and the fight for independence. *Evita* is about the life of Maria Eva Peron, Argentina's very popular first lady from the 1940s and 1950s, and an important figure in history.

In 1996, *Evita* was made into a movie starring Madonna as the title character. When they filmed in Argentina, Madonna stood in the same place the real Evita once stood as she gave her famous speech. For the musical, the speech becomes the song "Don't Cry for Me, Argentina." In interviews, Madonna said she felt a real connection to the history when she filmed that scene. The movie won an Academy Award in 1997 for the song "You Must Love Me." That song did not appear in the original play; it was written especially for the movie.

Andrew Lloyd Webber wrote the musical *Evita,* which, like *Jesus Christ Superstar,* has almost no spoken dialogue. This was considered European-style musical theater, different from the earlier musical comedies of America. *Evita* was the beginning of a huge series of successes for Andrew Lloyd Webber, who also wrote *Cats,* based on the poetry of T. S. Eliot, and *Joseph and the Amazing Technicolor Dreamcoat,* based on a biblical story.

Character Metaphors

This game will help you create a historical musical by creating scenes and/or songs. As you choose metaphors and act them out, your characters will really come to life.

Props

Pen

Paper

The musical *Annie Get Your Gun* is based on a real person named Annie Oakley who won a shooting contest against her husband.

Choose an event in history you would like to act out in a musical. Make a list of all the important characters in your musical. Now you're ready to use metaphors to help flesh out your characters.

A *metaphor* is when one object or phrase is used in place of another object or phrase to show the similarities between the two. In this game you'll use objects that remind you of or are similar to your character to help flesh him or her out. For example, you might say George Washington was like a tree because he was strong and grounded in the roots of America. Or, you might say Pocahontas was like the sun because she was warm, bright, and nurtured the earth. It's OK if you're not exactly sure why you choose your metaphor, as long as it reminds you of your character.

Walk around your acting space, then slowly become your metaphor. For example, the actor playing George Washington might plant his feet and spread his arms out like branches. Next, humanize your object; that is, let your object take on human characteristics. For example, the actor playing George Washington should become a human tree. Figure out how the object might walk and talk if it could. Now hold on to that feeling and become your character, preserving all the characteristics of the object.

Quickly take your pen and paper and complete the following sentences for your character.

I feel _____ because _____.

I do not like _____.

I do like _____.

I wish _____.

See if you can turn these short sentences into a monologue or a song. Share what you have written with others by taking turns reading your sentences aloud.

2

Musical Themes

There are musicals about almost everything, from people-eating plants (*Little Shop of Horrors*) to the French Revolution (*Les Misérables*), from orphan girls and boys (*Annie* and *Oliver*) to kings (*Camelot*) and first ladies (*Evita*).

This chapter divides some famous musicals by what they're about—their *theme*. Fairy-tale musicals, such as *Cinderella*, *Once Upon a Mattress*, and *Beauty and the Beast*; poetry musicals such as *Cats*; comic-strip musicals such as *Annie* and *You're a Good Man, Charlie Brown*; musicals inspired by Shakespeare such as *West Side Story* and *Kiss Me Kate*; book musicals such as *The Wizard of Oz* and *The King and I*; puppet musicals such as *Little Shop of Horrors*; and job musicals such as *Working* and *How to Succeed in Business Without Really Trying* are some of the musicals discussed here.

In this chapter you'll find activities and games that will help you get into the mood and learn more about the theme of each musical. This will be especially helpful if you will be performing in one of these musicals. These activities and games will also give you ideas to create your own theme musical. Even if you just enjoy playing, writing, or creating theater for fun in your own home or classroom, you will enjoy exploring the themes in this chapter.

There are character games in this chapter that will lead to creating and exploring different kinds of characters in a play, such as **Character Hat** and **Animal Characters**. If music is your thing, this chapter includes **Chanting Songs** and **Poems to Songs** to help you sing your way through different musical themes. Some of the games in this chapter also make excellent creative writing tools, such as **Write a Poem**, **Group Poems**, **Shakespeare Today**, and **Book Musicals**. If you are artistically inclined, you can make puppets to use in your play. For a great energy game, try **Kitty Wants a Corner**, and for a super party game be sure to try **Coffeepot**.

Fairy-Tale Musicals

Many musicals are based on fairy tales. Richard Rogers and Oscar Hammerstein wrote a musical version of *Cinderella*; *Once Upon a Mattress* is the musical version of the story *The Princess and the Pea*, and Disney's musical *Beauty and the Beast* is a classic fairy tale.

In the musical *Cinderella*, the prince's parents, the king and queen, take on a greater role than in the original fairy tale. You see them as parents concerned for the happiness of their son. The stepsisters get to sing a funny duet called "Why Would a Fellow Want a Girl Like Her," and Cinderella sings of how she daydreams in order to escape her hardships in the song "In My Own Little Corner."

A stage production of this story provides an interesting challenge: how do you turn a tattered dress into a beautiful ball gown before the audience's eyes? One way to do this is to toss the gown down from a *catwalk* (the catwalk is where the lights are hung in the space above the stage) so it appears to fall magically from the sky when the fairy godmother says the magic words. Another way to do it is to have the actor playing Cinderella wear her gown under her tattered dress, and make the tattered dress easy to remove so it can disappear quickly as the fairy godmother waves her wand. Sewing Velcro into the dress is a good way to make it come off quickly.

Once Upon a Mattress tells the story of *The Princess and the Pea* from the point of view of a minstrel who is visiting the kingdom. He serves as a narrator and a character in the story. In his opening song "Many Moons Ago," he tells the original story, then says that wasn't quite the way it happened.

Into the Woods combines *Cinderella*, *Rapunzel*, *Jack and the Beanstalk*, and *Little Red Riding Hood* into one big musical. It tells the story of what might happen if the characters from all of those tales met in the woods. To tie the stories together, the creators of *Into the Woods* made up another fairy tale about a baker and his wife who must break a witch's curse in order to have a child. To break the curse, they need to find the following objects from each of the other tales.

A cow as white as milk (Jack's cow)

A cape as red as blood (Little Red Riding Hood's cape)

Hair as yellow as corn (Rapunzel's hair)

A slipper as pure as gold (Cinderella's glass slipper)

As they go into the woods to find these objects, the audience sees how all of the fairy-tale characters interact.

The Jungle Book, *Beauty and the Beast*, and *The Lion King* are all animated Disney movies that were made into musicals for the stage. *The King and I* was done in the opposite order. It was a musical long before it became an animated movie.

Character Hat

Play this game to create ideas for your own fairy-tale musical! Act out characters from different tales and see how they interact.

Props
......

Pen

Paper

Hat or bowl

CHESHIRE CAT

PETER PAN

ALICE

DOROTHY

WENDY

Make a list of many different fairy-tale characters (at least one for each person playing the game). Tear each name off and drop it into a hat or bowl. Have everyone draw a character. Whatever character name you draw, that is who you will play in the game. Next, decide on a place where all of these characters might meet, such as the woods, a witch's dungeon, or a fairy party. Everyone then becomes his or her character and interacts with each other, pretending to be at the chosen place. Be sure to introduce yourself to everyone, and find out what the other character's lives are like. Which characters share things in common with you? For example, Wendy (from *Peter Pan*), Dorothy (from *The Wizard of Oz*), and Alice (from *Alice in Wonderland*) have all been to very magical places (Neverland, Oz, and Wonderland). They might have a lot to tell each other comparing adventures.

After everyone has had a chance to talk with one another, "take off" your character and discuss what happened during the game. See if you can create interesting scenes from your experiences.

Encore! Encore!

Try this game with themes other than fairy tales. Here are some ideas.

- ✦ Superheroes
- ✦ Presidents
- ✦ Children from different countries
- ✦ Cartoon characters

Play **Character Swap**. If you are in a play and have been rehearsing for a while (so that everyone knows the story and the characters pretty well), do a run-through with everyone playing a part other then their own. To be fair, put the name of each character in a hat or bowl and have everyone draw one to determine which part they will play. It's OK if you don't know the other character's lines; just improvise and do the best you can to get the basic point across in each scene.

This exercise will give you a chance to see how another person might portray your character. Also, it can be very funny to see someone else playing your role.

$16,000,000

The Broadway run of Disney's *Beauty and the Beast* cost $16 million to produce.

Chanting Songs

Chanting, or repeating the same lines to create a song, is used in many musicals. In *Into the Woods*, the baker and his wife don't want to forget the objects they must find, so they repeat them as part of a song:

> A cow as white as milk,
>
> A cape as red as blood,
>
> Hair as yellow as corn,
>
> A slipper as pure as gold.

In this exercise you can create your own chanting song.

 Think of four lines important to your character, and sing them over and over until they become a song.

For example, Alice from *Alice in Wonderland* might sing:

> I must follow that rabbit.
>
> That rabbit who is late.
>
> That rabbit who is white.
>
> I simply must find him.

While the caterpillar might sing:

> I'm a caterpillar,
>
> Exactly three inches tall.
>
> I smoke a pipe.
>
> Who are you?

And the Queen of Hearts could sing:

> Today we play croquet.
>
> I always win.
>
> Everyone must play,
>
> Or it's off with their head!

When three people have created their chanting songs, put them together. Each one sings their chant once separately, as if they each had a verse to sing. Then try singing them at the same time and see how it turns out.

Before writing music for such musicals as *Three Penny Opera*, Kurt Weill wrote a children's ballet called *Magic Night*.

Poetry Musicals

A Funny Thing Happened on the Way to the Forum takes place in ancient Rome, and is based on poems by the Roman poet Plautus. The costumes for this farce about a Roman slave who would like to have his freedom are togas. Stephen Sondheim composed the play's hit song, "Comedy Tonight," during the auditions.

Cats is a musical based on poetry by T. S. Eliot found in the book *Old Possum's Book of Practical Cats*. Andrew Lloyd Webber wrote the music, and the poems were used for the lyrics. Sometimes the poems are sung, and other times they are spoken in rhythm.

Many of the songs in *Cats* describe the characters, such as Grizabella the Glamour Cat, Rum Tum Tugger, and Old Deuteronomy.

The song "Memory" became the most popular song from *Cats*, and has been recorded by dozens of artists.

The actors in *Cats* study the movements of real cats to help get into character. The choreographer gets his inspiration from the way cats move, jump, pounce, and run.

Poems to Songs

Here are some ideas for making poems into songs.

 Try speaking some poems or nursery rhymes that you know in rhythm. Have someone keep the rhythm by clapping his or her hands or playing a small drum. Here's an example.

Jack and Jill

Went up the hill

To fetch a pail of water.

Jack fell down

And broke his crown

And Jill came tumbling after.

To market to market

To buy a fat pig.

Home again, home again

Jiggidy jig.

Peas porridge hot

Peas porridge cold

Peas porridge in the pot

Nine days old.

Home again, home again
Jiggidy jig.

Encore! Encore!

For a play that has poems in it that you can turn into songs, see *The Three Billy Goats Gruff* in the chapter titled "Show Time!"

Play **Throw It Out the Window**. Here's a funny song you can sing with nursery rhymes. Replace the last line of the nursery rhyme with the following song:

And threw it out the window

The window

The second-story window

High, low, low, high

Threw it out the window.

For example, the nursery rhyme "Old King Cole" would go like this:

Old king cole was a merry old soul

And a merry old soul was he

He called for his pipe, and he called for his bowl

And he threw them out the window

The window

The second-story window

High, low, low, high

Threw them out the window.

And here's how to sing "Humpty Dumpty" with this game:

Humpty Dumpty sat on a wall.

Humpty Dumpty had a great fall.

All the king's horses and all the king's men

Threw him out the window

The window

The second-story window

High, low, low, high

Threw him out the window.

School House Rock Live is a musical based on short cartoons that teach lessons about grammar, history, multiplication, and science.

Write a Poem

For ideas to create your own poetry musical, collect poems about a specific theme. You can write original poems yourself, or look in books of poetry.

T. S. Eliot chose cats for his theme. You might choose another animal, or any subject you like, such as nature, food, or sports. For a school musical, you could base your play on one of your school subjects and choose a scientific theme like planets, or a theme about a certain time in history, like the Renaissance.

There are a lot of different ways to write poems. Not all poems rhyme, but since these poems will become lyrics in your play, you'll probably want them to rhyme. In the nursery rhyme "Mary Had a Little Lamb," the second line rhymes with the fourth line:

1 Mary had a little lamb,

2 Her fleece was white as snow.

3 And everywhere that Mary went

4 Her lamb was sure to go.

The word "snow" rhymes with the word "go."

In some other poems, the first and second lines rhyme, and the third and fourth lines rhyme:

1 Georgie Porgie Pudding Pie

2 Kissed the girls and made them cry.

3 When the boys came out to play

4 Georgie Porgie ran away.

In this example, "pie" rhymes with "cry" and "play" rhymes with "away."

The musical *A Funny Thing Happened on the Way to the Forum* won the Tony Award for best play in 1963.

♫ *It is important to note that if you are using poems found in books, you may have to pay a royalty in order to perform them in your play.*

Group Poems

In this game you write poems in a group, one line at a time.

Props
Pens

Paper

Sit in a circle and choose one player to start. The player who starts makes up the first line of a poem, writes it down, and then passes it to the player on his right. The second player writes the second line to the poem and passes it to the person on her right, and so on, until four lines have been written. The fifth player reads the poem out loud.

Here's an example of how this game might work. Ben writes:

Trees can grow very tall

Ben passes the paper to Lauren, who writes:

But bushes can be very small.

Lauren passes the paper on to Alex who writes:

Birds can build their nests in trees

Alex passes the paper on to Todd who writes:

But beware of wasps and bees.

Todd passes the paper on to Kim who reads the entire poem out loud:

Trees can grow very tall

But bushes can be very small.

Birds can build their nests in trees

But beware of wasps and bees.

The subject they chose was trees, and they made lines one and two (tall and small) and lines three and four (trees and bees) rhyme.

Encore! Encore!

Instead of writing the poem down, try speaking it out loud. The first player says a line out loud, then the next player adds on, and so on. Try not to pause; just say the first thing that comes into your mind, even if it doesn't make perfect sense. Try to make the poem rhyme. You may want to have someone write down the poems as you go so you can use them in your musical.

Once you have practiced making up poems by saying your made-up line out loud, try doing it in rhythm. Have someone keep the rhythm by clapping or playing a drum or other rhythm instrument. Try to keep the rhythm going and make up a poem without pausing.

Richard Rodgers wrote his first song when he was 14 years old. When he was 16 he found his songwriting partner, Oscar Hammerstein.

Kitty Wants a Corner

Actors must warm up their bodies and focus their minds before starting to rehearse a play. To do this, they often start rehearsals with warm-up games that involve thinking, concentrating, and running around.

This is a warm-up game. Because you get to play a kitty, you'll get an additional benefit from playing this game if you are performing a play about cats.

 Stand in a circle. Choose one player to be the kitty. The kitty stands in the middle of the circle and faces someone who is standing in the circle. The kitty says, "Kitty wants a corner." The person they just spoke to says, "Go see my next-door neighbor," and points the kitty to her left or right. The kitty then goes to the next person in the direction she was told and says the same thing: "Kitty wants a corner." The new person says, "Go see my next-door neighbor," and points to his left or right. The kitty continues until she gets a "corner" or a place in the circle.

Here's how a space in the circle can open up. The rest of the players in the circle look around at each other. When eye contact is made between two players, they quickly trade places in the circle. To do this they run across the circle at the same time and take each other's places. When the kitty hears or sees this happening, she will also run and try to get one of these spaces. If she succeeds, the person left without a space is the new kitty.

There is no talking in this game, other than "Kitty wants a corner" and the response "Go see my next-door neighbor." There is no whispering or waving to communicate with someone that you'd like to change places. Just make eye contact and go.

Kitty wants a corner.

The musical *Rent* first opened in a theater that only had 99 seats. Now it plays to huge audiences all over the United States.

Animal Characters

The actors in *Cats* had to study cats to learn how to move like them. Try this character exercise to see what kinds of characters are like other animals.

Become an animal such as a horse by walking like a horse, moving your head like a horse, and making sounds like a horse. Next, make the horse a little more human, perhaps by having him walk on two legs, instead of four, but still keeping horselike movements and sounds. See if you can gradually make the horse sounds become more like a human's voice that sounds like a horse. Keep walking around as this half-horse/half-human character, and see if it reminds you of anyone. When you have someone in mind, turn into this person who is a lot like a horse. For example, you might trot instead of walk, nod your head a lot, and talk in a giggly but gruff voice. Imagine what kind of person does these things. Think of a name for yourself and a job that you do. For example, you might name your horse character Heather the cheerleader, or Joe the jockey. Go up to others and introduce yourself.

Continue this game with a number of different animals such as an elephant, goat, dog, pig, snake, fox, fish, or bird. See what different kinds of characters emerge.

Encore! Encore!

If you are working on a play, choose an animal that reminds you of your character. For example, the character of Lucy in *You're a Good Man, Charlie Brown* might remind you of a vulture because she's not very nice to people. Do a run-through of your play with everyone acting like the animal they have chosen. See how that helps to physicalize characteristics of your characters.

In *The Wizard of Oz* and *Annie* the dogs Toto and Sandy are played by dogs. But in *You're a Good Man, Charlie Brown*, Snoopy is played by a person who talks, sings, and dances.

Comic-Strip Musicals

My book report . . .

Annie and *You're A Good Man, Charlie Brown* are two musicals based on comic strips. In *Annie*, the comic-strip characters come together to create one story line for the musical. *You're A Good Man, Charlie Brown* is written like the actual comic strip: it has short scenes with punch lines at the end of each scene.

In the Broadway production of *Annie* there were 23 actors and three understudies, or "swing" actors (one man, one woman, and one girl), who could play the roles in case of illness. Even the dog, Sandy, had an understudy, named Arf. There were also 33 stagehands and 18 musicians.

The most popular song from *Annie* is "Tomorrow," which

Annie sings to cheer others up in difficult times. The song "Hard Knock Life" tells more about the difficult lives of these lovable orphans.

You're A Good Man, Charlie Brown is a much smaller musical, with only six characters: Charlie Brown, Snoopy, Linus, Lucy, Schroeder, and Patty. In one song, called "Book Report," four of the characters sing about their different strategies for writing book reports. Charlie Brown procrastinates, which means he puts off doing his homework until the last minute. His part of the song is about starting his book report tomorrow. Lucy knows that her book report must be 100 words long, so she is constantly counting words. She adds a lot of "very's" to her book report, even ending it with "the very, very, very end." Schroeder is supposed to write his book report on *Peter Rabbit*, but really loves the book *Robin Hood*. He sings about Robin Hood, then tries to tie it in with Peter Rabbit by saying the characters in Robin Hood run like rabbits. Linus is philosophical. He delves into the feelings of the characters in his book. At the end of the song, all four characters come together and sing their parts in four-part harmony.

In *You're A Good Man, Charlie Brown*, the costume for Snoopy is usually a white sweatshirt and jeans. The actor playing Snoopy doesn't wear a dog mask or costume. The audience knows he is Snoopy by the way he acts; this adds to the understanding that Snoopy thinks of himself as a person. The character of Snoopy can talk to the audience, but not to the other characters. He speaks only dog language, not human, but the audience can hear his thoughts.

 To create a musical like *You're a Good Man, Charlie Brown*, start by collecting a series of your favorite comic strips. Then try acting them out, turning each strip into a separate scene. See if you can group scenes together by themes, such as holidays or sports. To add music to your play, try to think of a special song for each character to sing. In your play, the scenes and songs can be separated by blackouts. A *blackout* is when the lights go out at the end of a scene. The lights come back up when the actors are in place for the next scene.

Woof woof!

Musicals Inspired by Shakespeare

Everything old is new again with plays that adapt classics. *Kiss Me Kate* is a musical based on the Shakespeare play *The Taming of the Shrew*, and *West Side Story* is based on *Romeo and Juliet*.

Kiss Me Kate is a play within a play. In the musical, the actors are rehearsing for a production of *The Taming of the Shrew* but their lives are similar to those of their characters. Shakespeare's lead character, Katharina, is played by the character Kate, and the one who tries to tame her, Petruchio, is played by the producer of the play.

In *West Side Story*, the saga of the star-crossed lovers in Romeo and Juliet is set in modern times. Instead of being from rival families as in the original Shakespearian play, the Capulets and the Montagues, they are from rival gangs, the Sharks and the Jets. They renamed the characters with modern names, too: Romeo, the son in the Montague family, becomes Tony, the leader of the Jets; Juliet, the daughter in the Capulet family, becomes Maria, whose brother is the leader of the Sharks; Mercutio, Romeo's best friend, becomes Rif, Tony's best friend; Thybolt, Juliet's cousin, becomes Bernardo, Maria's brother; the Nurse, who advises and helps Juliet, becomes Anita, Maria's older sister. In *West Side Story*,

the famous balcony scene from *Romeo and Juliet* takes place on a fire escape.

In the musical *The Fantasticks*, the story is the opposite of *Romeo and Juliet*. The parents of the young couple want them to fall in love and get married, and try to trick them into doing so.

The *Tony* is the name for the Broadway theater award, just like the *Oscar* for movies, the *Emmy* for television, and the *Grammy* for music.

Shakespeare Today

 Here's a way to create your own modern-day Shakespeare musical.

Choose a Shakespeare play, or one part of a play, to rewrite. Make it take place in the present. First, make sure you understand the play and the characters. Make a list of the main characters, and think of modern names for each of them. Then choose a modern place. For example, a king in a castle might become any of the following:

✦ The president in the White House

✦ A millionaire in a mansion

✦ A popular girl in her school

✦ A parent in a home

After you have your characters and location, see if you can make up experiences for them that somehow match the experiences in the original play. For example, in *West Side Story*, the masquerade ball becomes the dance party where Tony and Maria met. When the characters, places, and events are all changed, put it all together.

While based on the sad tale of *Romeo and Juliet*, there are funny moments in *West Side Story*, known as *comic relief*. Comic relief is when humor is put into a dramatic or sad story to give the audience some relief from the sadness. At one point the members of the Jets sing a funny song called "Gee, Officer Krupke," about what they'd like to say to a police officer.

The 1999 movie *Ten Things I Hate About You* is based on Shakespeare's *The Taming of the Shrew*.

Book Musicals

The Wizard of Oz was a book before it was a musical. *Really Rosie* is a musical based on a number of books by Maurice Sendak, and *The King and I* is based on the book *Anna and the King of Siam* by Margaret Landon. Many musicals began as books. Someone liked the book so much they decided to add music to it and create a play.

The King and I is based on the actual diaries of Anna Harriette Leonowens, who was a governess for King Mongkut of Siam from 1862 until 1867. The play and her diaries tell a lot about different cultures and how they conflict, but also about how they can learn to respect and help one another.

The Wiz is a musical based on the musical *The Wizard of Oz*, which in turn is based on the book of the same name by L. Frank Baum. William F. Brown, who wrote *The Wiz*, set the play in an imaginary ghetto with soul and disco music.

Really Rosie takes a number of Maurice Sendak books and transforms them into different songs and characters. The book *Chicken Soup with Rice* became the theme for Rosie's little brother, named Chicken Soup, and the books *One Was Johnny* and *A Alligators All Around* became songs for Rosie's friends, Johnny and Alligator (a boy who wears a hat shaped like an alligator).

Create a Book Musical

You can use any book for ideas to create a book musical but if you are going to perform this musical, you may want to choose carefully and consider a few questions: Where does the story in the book take place? Is it a set I can create? How many characters are in the book? Can I find that many actors or can some actors play more than one role?

Props

Paper

Pen

Choose a book that you want to turn into a musical. Make a list of the settings. For example, if you decided to adapt the book *Little Red Riding Hood*, the settings are the woods and Grandma's house. Next, make a list of the characters. The characters in this story include Little Red Riding Hood, the wolf, Grandma, and the hunter. Divide the story into scenes and/or beats. A *beat* is an event that happens in the play. A scene may include a number of beats. For example, a love scene may include a beat where the characters see one another, a beat where they proclaim their love, and a beat where they plan to meet again later. Here are the scenes and the beats within each scene for *Little Red Riding Hood*.

Scene 1

Little Red Riding Hood walks through the woods with her basket.

She meets the wolf.

He finds out where Grandma lives and tells Little Red Riding Hood to pick flowers.

Scene 2

The wolf runs ahead to Grandma's house, eats her, puts on her clothes, and gets into her bed.

Scene 3

Little Red Riding Hood arrives at Grandma's house, talks to the wolf, who she thinks is her Grandma, and discovers it's the wolf.

The wolf eats Little Red Riding Hood.

Scene 4

A hunter opens up the wolf and rescues Grandma and Little Red Riding Hood.

They sew rocks inside the wolf's stomach so he won't eat people ever again.

If you want, you can add scenes into your play that are not in the original book. For example, in the musical *Into the Woods*, a scene was added where Little Red Riding Hood goes to a bakery to buy the goodies to bring to Grandma. You could make up scenes about what happens after the story ends.

Make up dialogue, or lines, for the actors to say. There may already be dialogue in the book, such as:

LITTLE RED RIDING HOOD
Grandma, what big eyes you have!

WOLF
The better to see you with, my dear.

You can use these, make up your own, or use a combination of both. You can also add:

LITTLE RED RIDING HOOD
Grandma, what big feet you have!

WOLF
The better to dance with you, my dear.

One way to make up dialogue is to improvise the scene. Just make it up as you go! Have two actors pretend to be the wolf and Little Red Riding Hood and to meet each other in the forest. See if what they say would make good dialogue for your play.

Encore! Encore!
Play **Whose Point of View?** In the book *The True Story of the Three Little Pigs*, the traditional tale of *The Three Little Pigs* is told from the point of view of the wolf. Try retelling other famous stories from the point of view of other characters. Here are some ideas.

- Peter Rabbit from Mister MacGregor's point of view
- *Alice in Wonderland* from the White Rabbit's point of view
- *Robin Hood* from Maid Marian or the Sheriff of Nottingham's point of view
- *Jack and the Beanstalk* from the Giant's point of view
- *The Wizard of Oz* from Toto's point of view

The musical *Les Misérables* is based on the novel with the same name by Victor Hugo.

Puppet Musicals

Some musicals include both people and puppet characters telling the story of a play. In the Broadway musical version of *The Lion King*, puppets are used to create the animals, while the puppeteers sing and make the animals dance. In *Little Shop of Horrors*, a few different puppets are used to create a people-eating plant as it grows from a very small hand puppet to a giant puppet with an actor inside. Puppets are very important in *Little Shop of Horrors* because an actor can't grow from very little to very big in a two-hour play; but, you can use different size puppets to make it look like the plant grows.

Little Shop of Horrors is based on an old science-fiction movie about a people-eating plant. One of Jack Nicholson's first movie roles was in the original film; he played the dentist. In the movie of the musical, Steve Martin played the same role.

For the movie, Frank Oz, one of the creators of The Muppets and *Sesame Street*, created the puppets to play the plant.

The same songwriters for *Little Shop of Horrors* (Alan Menken and Howard Ashman) also wrote the music for Disney's *The Little Mermaid* and *Beauty and the Beast*.

Make a Cheshire Cat Puppet

One or more players

If you are performing *Alice in Wonderland*, you might choose to use a puppet for the Cheshire cat, since he appears and disappears as if by magic. Sometimes only parts of his body appear!

Props

Construction paper

Crayons or markers

Scissors

Large craft sticks

Glue

Large cloth or sheet

Gloves

Using crayons or markers, draw a picture of the Cheshire cat onto the construction paper. Cut your cat out and glue him to the top half of a craft stick. Leave the bottom half of the stick uncovered so you can hold the stick to make the cat move.

(Note: you may need more than one craft stick to support his round body.) Next make separate pictures of different parts of the cat: one picture of his tail, one of his body, one of his face, and one of just his smile. Glue each of these parts to a separate craft stick.

Once you are finished, act out a scene from *Alice in Wonderland* using your puppets. A musical with puppets is different from a puppet show because the puppets are acting along with human performers. Instead of using a puppet theater, the puppeteer may simply cover him- or herself in a large cloth and wear gloves. The audience sees the puppeteer, but they understand that the puppet is the character to watch.

Put a sheet over yourself and put on some gloves. If the sheet is not sheer enough to see through, ask an adult for an old sheet so that you can cut two holes for your eyes. This way you can see what you and all the other actors are doing.

Spread your puppets out nearby so you can quickly change which puppet you are holding. Start by holding the full puppet.

ALICE

Oh, hello! What a cute little cat.

(Puppeteer makes cat disappear.)

Where did you go? Here kitty, kitty, kitty.

(Puppeteer makes just the cat's face appear.)

PUPPETEER

Hello.

ALICE

Why are you smiling like that?

PUPPETEER

I am a Cheshire cat. All of us can smile and most of us do.

(Puppeteer makes the face disappear and only the smile appear.)

See?

ALICE

That is very curious. Can you point me toward the white rabbit?

(Puppeteer makes the smile disappear and only the tail appear.)

PUPPETEER

(pointing with the tail)

I believe he went that way, but you don't want to go that way. It's very scary.

(Puppeteer makes the tail disappear, and the body appear, shaking with fright.)

ALICE

What's so scary that way? A lion?

PUPPETEER

(The body disappears and the head appears shaking "no.")
No. Oh, my. It's much scarier than a lion.

ALICE

Is it a dragon?

PUPPETEER

(makes head disappear and whole self appear)
Oh, no. It's much scarier than a dragon.

ALICE

Well, what is it?

PUPPETEER

A hatter! Eeek!
(The cat disappears.)

ALICE

Wait! Come back! What's so scary about a hatter? They just make hats!

PUPPETEER

(just the head comes back)
He's mad.

ALICE

Well, I'll just tell him it's not polite to be angry all the time.

PUPPETEER

He's not mad like angry, he's mad like crazy.
(Puppeteer shakes the head in a crazy way.)

ALICE

I'm not afraid of a mad hatter. I'm going this way. Good-bye, Cheshire cat.

PUPPETEER

(makes the head disappear and just the smile appear)
Don't say I didn't warn you.

The title for the musical *Fiddler on the Roof* was taken from a painting by Marc Chagall.

Job Musicals

Working and *How to Succeed in Business Without Really Trying* are two musicals about jobs.

In *Working*, based on Studs Terkel's book of the same name, interviews with different workers become monologues and songs. The paperboy sings about his favorite part of his job—throwing the paper in the bushes and watching as the bushes shake.

How to Succeed in Business Without Really Trying, based on a novel by Shepherd Mead, follows the character J. Pierpont Finch as he works his way to the top in his company. One way he does this is to sing his boss's college fight song with him. At the time of this musical, most musicals were about love stories, but the ambitious Finch's main love song, "I Believe in You," is sung to himself in the bathroom mirror.

Frederick Loewe was a boxer, a mail carrier, and a gold digger before becoming a composer for musical theater.

Coffeepot

In the musical *How to Succeed in Business Without Really Trying*, there is a song called "Coffee Break." All of the office workers sing about their favorite time of day—when it's time to take a coffee break. It is a funny number because it exaggerates the characters' love for coffee. The characters act silly, as if coffee were a wonderful friend.

This warm-up game helps actors focus and concentrate, as well as communicate with each other. It's a guessing game, only instead of saying the action you are trying to guess, you have to say "coffeepot."

 Send one player out of the room. While she is gone, decide on an action, such as chewing gum. Then have the player come back into the room. She has to guess what the action is. She asks questions to help her guess what the action is, but since she doesn't know what the action is, she calls it "coffeepotting." She might ask:

Who here has ever coffeepotted before?

Anyone who has ever chewed gum should raise his or her hand.

Then she might ask individual questions to players such as:

How often do you coffeepot?

Do you enjoy coffeepotting?

Have we ever coffeepotted together?

The questions don't have to be yes or no questions, but the other players can refuse to answer on the grounds that it might give it away.

The game continues until the guesser has figured out what the coffeepot is.

Here are some ideas for coffeepots.

- ✦ Baking cookies
- ✦ Hitting a home run
- ✦ Getting your ears pierced
- ✦ Flying on an air plane
- ✦ Square dancing
- ✦ Reading a book

This is also a terrific party and travel game.

The producer of *No, No, Nanette* convinced writer Vincent Youmans to add the famous song "Tea for Two" to his musical. "I Want to Be Happy" is another famous song from that musical.

3

Musical Reviews

A *review* is a show featuring a variety of songs, dances, and skits, which all reflect a common theme. Stephen Sondheim's musical *Follies* is based on Broadway reviews.

If you want to create your own show, one way to do it is to pick a theme and gather songs, dances, and scenes around that theme. You could begin by choosing a fun song about a special theme, and use that song for the title of your show. Here are some examples.

✦ "Under the Sea" from The Little Mermaid

could be the theme for a show about fish, mermaids, and other sea creatures. You could make fish puppets to perform with and decorate your set with giant fish cutouts. You could sing and dance to many songs, including "Octopus's Garden" and "Yellow Submarine" by the Beatles, or even find music that has whale sounds for a modern dance. You could make up scenes for characters such as mermaids, sea monsters, deep-sea divers, and even starfish and seaweed. To do research and find ideas, you could visit an aquarium or read books about the ocean.

✦ The song "Monster Mash" could be the theme song for a show about different kinds of monsters, including Dracula, Frankenstein, and the Wolfman. You could make scary monster masks and decorate your set like a haunted house complete with cobwebs made from string. You could dance to music from scary movies and sing "The Purple People Eater." You could make up scenes about where the monsters come from and what they like to do. You could research your monster theme by going to the library and looking for both funny and scary monster books.

✦ The song "Take Me Out to the Ball Game" could be the theme song for a show about sports. Your costumes could be uniforms and baseball caps, and you could sing and dance to the theme songs and fight songs of your favorite teams. Scenes could teach your audience about good sportsmanship.

You can also build your review by picking a place and choosing performance pieces that complement this theme. Here are some ideas.

✦ A review with a beach theme might include songs by the Beach Boys and your costumes could be sunglasses and bathing suits.

✦ A review with a jungle theme could include songs such as "The Lion Sleeps Tonight," by Robert John, and ideas from Rudyard Kipling's *The Jungle Book* and books of African folk tales.

✦ A review with a circus theme could include juggling, acrobatics, and other skills. You can use circus music or songs such as "Be a Clown" and "Send in the Clowns."

You could also choose your theme based on a decade. Here are some ideas.

✦ A 1950s theme might include music by Elvis, and the costumes could be poodle skirts or white T-shirts and jeans with the cuffs rolled up.

✦ A 1960s theme could include tie-dyed clothes and Beatles songs. You could make beaded necklaces and decorate your set with beaded curtains, too.

✦ For a 1970s show, you might decorate the stage to look like a discotheque, complete with a disco ball, bell-bottom pants, and dance to songs like "YMCA."

For scripts of short plays that have the same theme, see "Show Time!", where you'll find three plays about American folk heroes.

You may need to pay royalties to use the music in your review. There is an organization called the American Society of Composers, Authors, and Publishers (ASCAP) that can tell you if you will need a royalty contract.

The Richard Rodgers and Lorenz Hart musical *Babes in Arms* is about kids who decide to put on their own show.

Three-Part Characters

You can create crazy and unusual characters by playing this artistic game. Choose a theme such as monsters, animals, or superheroes, or just let everyone make whatever comes to mind. You draw one part of the character (his top, middle, or bottom) and other players draw the other parts, without seeing what you have drawn. Very unusual characters can be created this way.

Props
Paper

Markers, crayons, or colored pencils

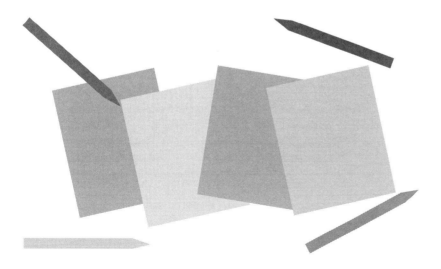

Sit in a circle. Each player takes a piece of paper and folds it into thirds as if you were going to put it into an envelope. Each player draws the head of a person, creature, or character on the top third of the paper. When finished, draw a couple of marks on the middle third of the paper to show the next person where he is to begin drawing. Fold the top third down so that the head you drew is not showing and only the middle third of the paper is on top. When each player is through, pass your paper to the person sitting on your right. On the paper you receive, draw the middle of any type of person, creature, or character. Use the marks drawn for you by the previous player as your guide. You should draw something completely different from the head you drew on the other piece of paper.

After you finish drawing the middle section, fold the paper again and make a few marks in the bottom third to help guide the person who will draw this last part of the figure. Be sure to fold it so only the bottom part is showing. Pass the paper to your right. Now draw the bottom of any type of person, creature, or character on the piece of paper passed to you. It can have two feet, four feet, or any kind of bottom you like. It can even have wheels, or the end of the tail of a snake. Connect it to the marks left for you by the previous player. Pass the paper one more time.

Open the paper that you are handed. See what sort of crazy character the three of you have created together. The head, middle, and bottom won't match because you didn't know what others had drawn when you drew your part. Make up a name for this crazy character. For example, if it has a horse head, a fire-fighter's middle, and duck feet, you could name it Fiery Quackhorse. Go around the circle and introduce each character to everyone else by showing the picture and saying the character's name. Each group can introduce their character or each person can introduce her third of the character.

Encore! Encore!

After you have created these three-part characters, act them out. Pretend to be Fiery Quackhorse and meet the other characters.

Fred Astaire played the title role in the movie version of the musical *Finian's Rainbow*. Based on a Celtic fairy tale, the movie also featured a goblin character named Og.

Talking Stick

Once you have chosen a theme, this exercise is one way to create an original scene. You can put everyone's thoughts on your theme together to create a scene written by the entire group.

Props
Rain stick, walking stick, or a unique stick found outside

Pen

Paper

 Sit in a circle and take some time to discuss the theme of your show. Talk about what objects, pictures, and other things are related to your theme. If you plan ahead, you can bring objects and pictures to show others in your group. For example, if your theme is a certain country, such as Africa, show some photographs from books on Africa and pass around an African mask and drum.

Next, take out the stick. A rain stick is a stick that is filled with seeds and makes a sound like rain when you turn it upside down. If you have a rain stick, use it as your talking stick. If not, any stick will do. (If you would like to make a rain stick, see **Make a Musical Instrument** in "I've Got Rhythm" for instructions, but instead of a toilet-paper roll, use a wrapping-paper roll.)

The stick is called the talking stick because the person who is holding the stick does the talking. Everyone else listens. Choose one player to go first and give him the stick. He says, "When I think of _____ (your theme), I think of _____," and says whatever comes to mind. For example, he might say, "When I think of Africa, I think of the jungle." He then passes the talking stick to the player on his left, who says, "When I think of Africa, I think of _____," and fills in the blank.

It's OK to repeat what someone else has said. If you have time to plan ahead and can share pictures and/or objects related to your theme, then participants who didn't already have something in mind could get some ideas from these objects.

Have someone write down what everyone says as the stick is being passed around the circle.

The next step is to divide what everyone said into subjects. For example, everyone who said they thought of the rain forest, animals, or plants will form one group. Those who said they thought of cultural things, such as masks and drums, make another group. Have the groups get together and make up a short scene about their topic. The scene should begin with the line: "When I think of Africa, I think of _____," then list all of the things said in their topic as members of each group act them out. After each group has created a scene, put them together into one big scene for your review.

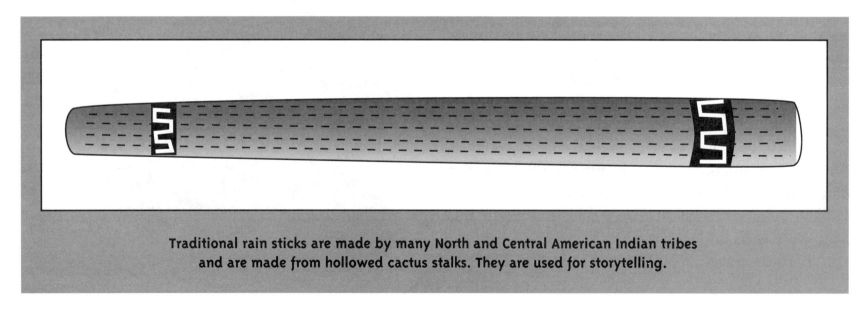

Traditional rain sticks are made by many North and Central American Indian tribes and are made from hollowed cactus stalks. They are used for storytelling.

Story Cards

Ever heard of writer's block? That's when a writer is having trouble thinking of ideas for things to write about. In this game questions are used to help everyone think of ideas for scenes and to stomp out writer's block.

Props

Index cards

Pens

 To create scenes to go into your theme variety show, write down ideas for telling stories on separate index cards. For example, if your theme is countries, you can tell all kinds of stories.

Here are some ideas.

+ A plane or train ride you have taken
+ A time when you didn't understand the language someone was speaking
+ A time when you went to another country
+ A country you'd like to visit and why
+ The country your family is from
+ A time when you tried food from another country
+ Something you own that was made in another country

For a monster theme show, you can tell a story about:

+ A time when you dressed up in costume
+ A time when you were scared
+ Ghosts
+ A scary movie you saw
+ Something you did on Halloween
+ Your favorite monster
+ A haunted place

If there are a lot of players, divide into groups of four or five. Give each group at least three different index cards. Read the cards in your group and have everyone tell a story that one of the cards reminds them of. If you'd like, have someone write down the stories, so you can remember them to create scenes later. After everyone in the group has told at least one story, choose one of the stories to act out. Make up a scene acting out that story. Rehearse it a few times in your group, then show it to the other players.

There is a board game called *Life Stories* that provides story cards
to inspire families to play together and learn about one another.

Spelling Scenes

If you have chosen a theme with a one-word title, this game is a great way to make up an original scene for your variety show. Using the letters in the word of your theme, you can create a unique scene for your show or just for fun.

Props

Pen

Paper

 Sit in a circle, and choose one player to write down what everyone says. Start with the first letter of your theme. For example, if your theme is circus, start with the letter C, and think of all the things or phrases having to do with a circus that start with the letter C. Then continue with each letter. If a letter is said more than once, such as C in circus, be sure to come up with at least two things that start with that letter.

Here are some examples.

C	clowns, costumes, crowd
I	"in the center ring"
R	roar of lions, ringmaster, rides on elephants
C	cotton candy, children
U	"under the big top"
S	sideshow

Next, divide into as many groups as there are letters in your word. For circus, divide into six groups and assign each group a letter. Each group will make up a scene about their letter.

Each group chooses one player to pose as their letter. She makes the shape of that letter with her body. The group begins by saying, "C is for _____," and listing all of the things starting with C (in the case of circus, the C words are divided between the two Cs) while acting them out. You can put words together into a sentence, such as "clowns wearing costumes."

After each group has made up a scene, take turns performing your scene in the order that the letters appear in your theme's word. You can choose a narrator to speak the lines as they are being acted out, or divide the lines up so that they can be said by the actor acting them out. At the end of all of the scenes, the letter-posing people line up and make the whole word while everyone spells it out.

Here's an example of how this exercise might work.

● ●

FIRST C GROUP

(A person from the first C group poses like the letter C.)
C is for clowns wearing funny costumes.
(Now members of the first C group act like clowns.)
And a huge crowd formed.
(First C group acts like a crowd.)

I GROUP

(A person from the I group poses like the letter I.)
I is for the interesting acts in the center ring.
(I group acts out performances you see in the center ring.)

R GROUP

(A person from the R group poses like the letter R.)
R is for the ringmaster who makes the lions roar,
(Someone from the R group acts as the ringmaster working with roaring lions.)
and for riding on the back of elephants.
(R group acts out an elephant ride.)

SECOND C GROUP

(A person from the second C group poses like the letter C.)
C is for cute children chewing cotton candy.
(C group acts like children eating cotton candy.)

U GROUP

(A person from the U group poses like the letter U.)
U is for the unbelievable acts under the big top.
(U group acts out the acts under the big top.)

S GROUP

(A person from the S group poses like the letter S.)
S is for the silly sideshow.
(S group acts out sideshow acts.)

ALL

(All posing people stand together, in order, to spell out circus.)
C-I-R-C-U-S spells circus!

● ●

The musical *Barnum* is about the life story of Phineas Taylor ("P.T.") Barnum, who started Barnum and Bailey's circus.

4

A Performer Prepares

~~~~~~~~~~~~~~~~~~~~~~~~~~~~~~~~

The life of a professional musical actor is a lot of work. An actor goes on many more auditions than the number of roles he or she is offered. When an actor does make a play, he or she rehearses long hours for many weeks. An actor must memorize his or her lines and work with the director to develop his or her character in the play and learn the blocking (movement onstage). An actor is fitted for a costume. They are taught what makeup is necessary for the role and how to apply it for performances under hot lights. But when an actor takes his or her bow at the curtain call and hears the applause from the audience, he or she knows that all the hard work was worth it.

On the night of a performance actors arrive at least a half hour before show time. The time that they are asked to arrive is called the *actor's call*. Actors often arrive earlier if they must apply a lot of makeup or wear a complex costume. Just before *curtain*, when the show begins, the stage manager calls out "places" and everyone goes to his or her place for the start (sometimes referred to as the top) of the show. When not onstage, actors wait in what is called the "green room." It doesn't have to be painted green. That's just what they call a room where actors who are not onstage can sit and relax while they wait for their cue.

When Andrea McArdle played the role of Annie on Broadway, she had a pinball machine in her dressing room.

Auditions

Deciding who will play what part is called *casting*. In order to cast a play, the director holds auditions. When you audition for a musical there are usually three parts to the audition—singing, dancing, and acting. Often, actors are asked to prepare two songs for their singing audition—an upbeat or fast song, and a ballad or slow song. Actors sing only a short part of each song (usually 12 bars of music or about one minute). They bring their own sheet music and give it to the piano player at the audition to play.

A common question actors have is whether or not they should sing a song from the play they are auditioning for. Usually directors prefer if actors do not because directors do not want to hear the same songs over and over. On the other hand, directors may want to hear a song from the play to make sure the actor can sing in a specific character's range. For example, at auditions for the play version of *The Wizard of Oz*, girls auditioning were asked to sing "Somewhere Over the Rainbow," but for the movie *Annie*, girls auditioning were told they could sing any song except "Tomorrow."

For the dance audition, the choreographer (the person who stages the dances in the play) will often hold a dance clinic. At the dance clinic the actors learn a short dance. They then show the choreographer the dance they have learned. If there is a dance clinic, actors wear dance clothes to the audition.

Even if there is not dancing in the play, actors usually go to auditions dressed in professional but comfortable clothes that enable them to move around easily.

Los Angeles is known as the "City of Angels," which is where the musical of the same title got its name.

Tempo Game

In this game, you will find funny ways to sing your favorite songs and to practice the difference between up-tempo songs and slow ballads.

 Pick a song that everyone knows, such as "Take Me Out to the Ball Game." Select one player to be the conductor. Begin singing the song and keep your eyes on the conductor. When the conductor's arms are up, players should sing fast or up-tempo. When the conductor's arms are down, players should sing slowly, like a ballad. See if the song sounds happier when it's fast and sadder when it's slow.

Encore! Encore!

Try playing the **Tempo Game** with the conductor pointing to individuals to sing solo. When the conductor points to a player, he begins the song. The conductor may have him sing fast or slow. Then she may point to another player. The second player continues the song exactly where the first player left off, remembering to watch the conductor for the correct tempo.

It took Rodgers and Hammerstein just 10 minutes to write the song "Oh, What a Beautiful Morning" for the musical *Oklahoma*.

Dance Clinic

Many choreographers will include basic standard steps to see how well the actors can dance. You can make up your own dance audition with this activity.

 Find some music that is fun to dance to, then make up a few steps that you think will show off how well you can dance. Try to include at least three of the following:

Leap

Turn

Skip

Walking in rhythm (to the music playing)

Cartwheel

Spin

End your dance with a big dramatic pose.

You don't have to be a great dancer to have a great dance audition. The most important things to remember are to look up and smile!

In *West Side Story*, the musical number "The Rumble" uses dance to show two gangs in a fight. A famous choreographer, Jerome Robbins, choreographed *West Side Story* for Broadway.

Cold Reading

For the acting audition, many actors have monologues prepared. Just like with their songs, actors will usually have two different monologues, each around two minutes long. They might have one monologue from a classic play by Shakespeare and another from a modern or contemporary play. Or they might have one funny and one serious monologue.

Another kind of acting audition is called *cold reading*, or reading from the script. The actors are given *side*s (a few pages or a short scene) from a script. The actors read the sides out loud in front of the director, doing the best they can to act out the character as they read their part. After an actor has read his sides, the director might give him some direction (to read the text a different way or focus on an idea) and then ask the actor to reread the side.

You can practice your cold reading skills with this game.

Props
Book

Choose one player to be the actor and one to be the director. The director chooses a short page or paragraph in a book and gives it to the actor. The actor reads it out loud. Then the director asks the actor to read it again in a different way. The director might choose:

* Sleepy
* Loud
* Rushed
* Romantic
* Sneaky
* Old

The actor then adjusts his reading of the same page or paragraph using the direction given.

The best practice for cold-reading auditions is reading out loud every day. Read a book, newspaper, or even billboards you see while driving in the car. Read the same thing several different ways.

Animal Crackers and *Coconuts* were plays written for the Marx Brothers. The musical *Minnie's Boys* was written about the Marx Brothers and their mother, who took them to auditions and encouraged them to get into show business.

Wonderland Warm-Ups

An actor warms up his body and voice before an audition. In order to make these warm-ups fun, you can create your own silly movements and sounds. You will get a good warm-up as long as your movements are active and you use different sounds to warm up your voice. Because the land Alice visits in *Alice in Wonderland* is so crazy, this crazy game is called **Wonderland Warm-Ups**.

 Stand in a circle and choose one player to go first. That player does a warm-up sound and movement four times. For example, she may do four jumping jacks while counting to four. Next, the person to her left makes up a sound and movement and does it four times, such as wiggling his arms and saying "doodly-doo." Put the first two together:

One, two, three, four
(while doing jumping jacks)

Doodly-doo, doodly-doo, doodly-doo, doodly-doo
(while wiggling your arms).

The next person adds on his part of the warm-up, such as marching forward four steps, then back four steps while saying "hut" with each step. Put all three together:

One, two, three, four
(while doing jumping jacks)

Doodly-doo, doodly-doo, doodly-doo, doodly-doo
(while wiggling your arms)

Hut, hut, hut, hut, hut, hut, hut, hut
(while marching forward and back).

The fourth person adds on more movements and sounds, perhaps crossing her arms, kicking her feet, and saying, "hey, hey, hey." Put the whole thing together:

One, two, three, four
(while doing jumping jacks)

Doodly-doo, doodly-doo, doodly-doo, doodly-doo
(while wiggling your arms)

Hut, hut, hut, hut, hut, hut, hut, hut
(while marching forward and back)

Hey, hey, hey, hey, hey, hey, hey, hey
(while kicking your feet).

Once you have created your own **Wonderland Warm-Ups**, write them down and start each rehearsal with them.

For a scene from *Alice in Wonderland* to use with your **Wonderland Warm-Ups**, see the chapter titled "Show Time!"

In Disney's *Cinderella*, the fairy godmother sings "Bibbidi, Bobbidi, Boo," while in the Rodger's and Hammerstein version she sings "Impossible." The song teaches Cinderella that things you think are impossible might actually happen if you believe that they can.

Vocal Warm-Ups

In addition to physical warm-ups, actors also warm up their voices for singing and for speaking loud and clear. In *My Fair Lady*, there is a scene where the lead character is trying to learn to speak proper English. She practices by singing the song "The Rain in Spain."

Singing in the Rain is a musical about actors who must learn to go from silent-movie acting to acting in talking pictures, called "talkies" at the time. A vocal coach is hired and one of the tongue twisters he teaches is in the song "Moses Supposes His Toeses Are Roses."

 You can use any of your favorite tongue twisters to help warm up your voice, and singing the scales is a good way to warm up your singing voice. Here are some suggestions for vocal warm-ups.

Say these warm-ups out loud.

> *Whether the weather is cold,*
> *Whether the weather is hot,*
> *We'll be together, whatever the weather,*
> *Whether we like it or not.*
>
> *Remember the money,*
> *Remember the money,*
> *Remember the money,*
> *Remember.*
>
> *A dragon will come when he hears the drum*
> *At a minute or two 'til two today,*
> *At a minute or two 'til two.*

Here are some singing warm-ups.

Do re me fa so la te do
(Follow the notes of music like in the song "Do-Re-Mi" from *The Sound of Music*.)

Ma may me mo moo
(Then replace the M with other consonants, such as P, B, and D.)

Here are a couple of phrases that use a variety of vowel sounds.

Open-pit barbecue sauce

Oh, what a beautiful day

The musical *My Fair Lady* won the Tony Award for best play in 1957.

Yo Ho Ho

In *The Pirates of Penzance*, an orphan boy gets to work on a pirate ship. He falls in love with a girl named Mabel, whose dad is a major general in the army. The song he sings, "I Am the Model of a Modern Major General," is a tongue twister that is so difficult to say actors use it to warm up their voices before performing.

 You can create your own musical about pirates. Here is a pirate song where you fill in the blanks and make up the movements.

When I was one I _____.
(Fill in the blank with something that rhymes with one, such as "had some fun.")

The day we went to sea

I climbed on board the pirate ship

And the captain said to me

Go this way, that way, back again

Over the Irish sea.

A bottle of rum to tickle my tum

It's the pirate's life for me.

Yo Ho Ho.

Repeat with "When I was two," and so on through the number 10.

Be sure to add movements, especially for the "this way, that way, back again" part.

Real-life pirate Bluebeard did not actually have a blue beard, but he did set his beard on fire in order to scare others.

A Song for A

Alliteration is when words are put together in a song or sentence that start with the same letter. Many song writers use alliteration in their songs because it sounds melodic and is fun to sing. Here is an idea for a song or vocal warm-up game that uses alliteration.

 Start singing or chanting:

A A A

Here's a song for A.

Then make up a line using words that start with the letter A, such as:

Ants acting acrobatics.

A A A

B B B

Here's a song for B.

Then make up a line using words that start with the letter B, such as:

Bubbles become bubble gum.

B B B

Try it for every letter in the alphabet.

See if you can think of the alliterations without planning them in advance. Just say whatever comes to mind, and try to stay in the rhythm of the song.

Encore! Encore!

Play **Circle Alliteration**. If you have a group of people, stand in a circle and take turns. For example, choose a person to begin. She has the letter A. After she says her four lines of the song, the person to her right sings about B, and so on.

> My home thweet home!

The song "Gary, Indiana" was written by Meredith Wilson for the musical *The Music Man*. It was sung by a little boy who wanted a song without a lot of S's in it because he had a lisp.

Play **Alliteration Ball**. Bounce a ball while you sing the song to help you keep the rhythm. Then toss the ball to someone else who must take the next letter.

Play **Sign Alliteration**. Learn how to do the alphabet in sign language. Then make the sign for each letter when you sing that letter.

Name Ball

When actors begin working on a play together, one of the first things they must do is get to know one another. This is a name game that also involves some memorization and focus.

Props
• • • • • •
Ball

 Stand in a circle. Toss the ball to someone and say her name. She then tosses the ball to someone else, saying his name. Continue until everyone has been tossed the ball one time. Pass the ball around again in the exact same order. Keep passing the ball in that order, and see how fast you can go without anyone dropping the ball. Next, pass the ball in the opposite order. See if everyone remembers who passed the ball to them. See how fast you can go in the opposite order.

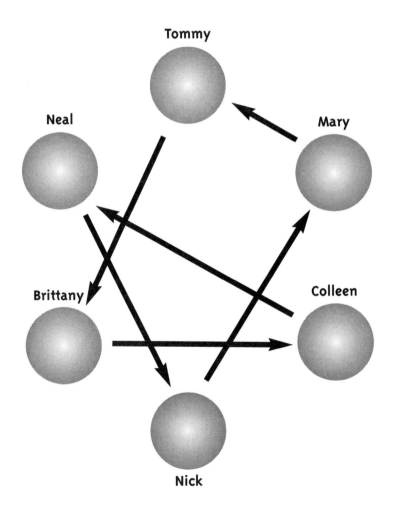

Encore! Encore!

Play **Racing Name Ball**. Divide into groups. (Each group should have an even number of people, at least six per group.) After the ball has been tossed around once, and the order has been established, have a race. See which group can pass it around in the same order again. Then race going in reverse order. For example, let's say there are two teams.

Each team tosses the ball once around, saying the name of the person they are tossing it to in order to establish the order. Then someone says, "On your mark, get set, go!" Each team then quickly tosses the ball in the same order again. When the ball comes back to the person who started, the team cheers to let the other team know they won the race. After a few races in that order, try it backwards.

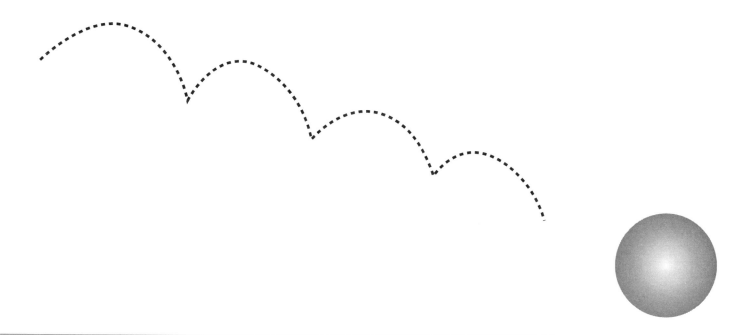

Big River is a musical based on Mark Twain's *The Adventures of Huckleberry Finn*. Mark Twain's real name was Samuel Clemens.

Memorizing Your Lines

Memorizing lines is an important job for actors. There are some tricks to memorizing. For example, you might know a trick for memorizing the names of the planets by how close they are to the Sun. If you can remember a sentence where each word starts with the same letter as each of the planets, it will help you remember. Here's an example.

Martha visits every Monday and just stays
until noon period.

Martha (Mercury)

Visits (Venus)

Every (Earth)

Monday (Mars)

And (asteroids)

Just (Jupiter)

Stays (Saturn)

Until (Uranus)

Noon (Neptune)

Period (Pluto)

Another trick for memorizing is to make a word or name using the first letters of the things you're trying to remember. For example, many people remember the colors of the rainbow by thinking of the name Roy G. Biv:

R (red)

O (orange)

Y (yellow)

G (green)

B (blue)

I (indigo)

V (violet)

Memorization can be easy when there is a poem or song to help you remember. Here's a poem to help you remember a grammar rule.

I before E

Except after C

Or when sounding like A

As in neighbor and sleigh.

Usually actors can't rely on these tricks because they don't have time to think of sentences, names, or poems before they say their lines. But there are other tricks actors use. Here are some of them.

◆ Read your script every day.

◆ Read your script out loud making different voices for the different characters.

◆ Have someone "run lines" with you. This means they hold the script and read the line before yours. (This is called your "cue line.") You say your line, and they tell you if you are right or wrong.

◆ If there is no one to run lines with you, tape record the other character's lines, leaving space on the tape for you to practice your lines when you play the tape back.

The song "Try to Remember" is from the musical *The Fantasticks. The Fantasticks* opened Off-Broadway and ran for over 35 years with around 15,000 performances.

We've got to cross the river by nine o'clock.

◆ Think of funny pictures in your head. For example, if your line is, "We've got to cross the river by nine o'clock," you might imagine drawing an X over a river next to the number nine.

◆ Think of ways to connect your cue line to your line. Your cue line is the line that comes before your line. For example, if your cue line is, "That girl's hair is so red," and your line is, "We'd better get ready to go," you might remember that when the other actor says "red," you say "ready."

◆ Stay in character. If you really know your character and the story of the play, it is easier to remember what your character would say.

◆ Practice your lines and your blocking at the same time. Sometimes it's easy to remember what your line is when you think of where you are when you say it.

Memory Ball

This game is for when you are rehearsing for a play production and everyone has begun to memorize his or her lines. It's great practice, because you not only have to know your own line, but also who has the lines before and after you.

Props
Ball

Sit in a circle. The person who has the first line holds the ball. The first person says her line, then passes the ball to the person she thinks has the next line. If

she is mistaken, the ball is tossed back to her, and she tries again. If she is correct, the person who caught the ball says his line, tosses it to the person he thinks has the next line, and so on.

Rules
1. You may only speak if you have the ball.
2. If you know your line is next, just wait. Don't give it away by reaching for the ball before it's tossed.
3. If you know who has the next line, don't say. If the ball is tossed to you, and it's not your line, just toss it back. The person tossing it must figure it out, even if it means tossing it to every single cast member.

Encore! Encore!
Try playing **Memory Ball** with your blocking. While you are walking onstage in your scene, toss the ball to the other characters just like before. See if acting in character causes you to throw the ball differently to different characters. For example, if you are acting angry, see if you throw the ball harder than when you are acting happy.

The musical *Damn Yankees* is about a man who sells his soul to the devil so he can play professional baseball.

An Actor Remembers

There are some basic rules in theater that an actor generally follows.

Don't turn your back to the audience or upstage other actors.

With few exceptions, the audience should always be able to see the front of you. That way they can see your facial expressions as you act, and your voice will carry out into the crowd.

Just as you must not turn your back to the audience, you must also make sure you don't block anyone else onstage from being seen by the audience. If you stand right in front of someone, it makes a poor stage picture. Be sure to leave room between actors so the audience can see everything that is happening onstage. If you are downstage (closer to the audience) you may want to sit or kneel so you don't block anyone behind you. If you are upstage (further away from the audience) be sure to stand straight and tall so you can be seen.

Always speak loud and clear.

No matter how well you know your lines, or how good of an acting job you are doing, it won't make any difference if the audience can't hear or understand you. Actors do a lot of enunciation exercises, such as tongue twisters and breathing exercises—like Mrs. Sadie in "I Got Rhythm"—as theatrical speaking voice warm-ups.

Use good posture and don't shuffle your feet.

Slouching doesn't look very good onstage. If you are singing in a musical, it is especially important to stand up straight. It helps you sing out and loud. Shuffling your feet makes it look like you're not sure where you're going. Plant your feet (keep them still on the ground) until it is time to walk somewhere. Then walk there with a purpose, and when you get there, plant your feet again.

Another important thing to remember about your posture is how you sit. While it may be proper now for women to cross their legs, it used to be proper for them to cross their ankles instead. Make sure you know how your character would sit in her time period.

In order to practice these acting rules, play this game. Be prepared to get silly! When you break a rule you have to continue the scene, but your penalty is to do silly things while you act, like hop on one foot, or hold your ear.

> Broadway has been the major American theater district since 1830.

Props

Scene from a play

 To start this game, you will need a scene to act out. It can be a scene from a play you are working on, or you can improvise and make it up as you go. If you are improvising, decide on **who** (your characters), **what** (an action), and **where** (the location of your scene).

Begin acting your scene, but be sure to follow the rules. Whenever you break a rule, you must pay the penalty. That means doing something silly for the rest of the scene.

If you turn your back to the audience:

once, then hold one hand up high;

twice, then hop on one foot; or

three times, then do the booty scoot. That means sit on the ground and scoot your way around the stage, keeping that one hand up.

If you mumble or talk too softly:

once, then hold your ear;

twice, then hold your other ear; or

three times, then twist your body back and forth (still holding both ears).

If you use poor posture or shuffle your feet:

once, then hold one elbow up in the air;

twice, then hold the other elbow up in the air; or

three times, then flap your elbows like a chicken.

You can make up funny penalties for other rules that may be important to your show, such as:

✦ Smiling during dances

✦ Remembering your lines

✦ Not cracking up or laughing when you're not supposed to

✦ Not looking down or at others during dances

✦ Singing loudly

Blocking a Musical

Blocking is an important job of the director. She has to make sure all of the movements make sense, but also that they make a good stage picture. Sometimes in a play, blocking problems come up that are difficult to solve.

If you were directing a production of *Little Red Riding Hood*, how would you make it look like the wolf eats Grandma and Little Red Riding Hood? Later, how would you make it look like the hunter gets them out? There are many different ways it can be done, and it's the director's job to decide which way to use.

In this case she might work with the set designer to come up with a way to use the bed. Perhaps the bed could be built large enough for the two actors to hide in. If there was a large hole in the bed, they could go into the hole while pretending to be eaten, then jump out of it when they are saved. If you could not build a bed, perhaps you could find one large enough for the actors to hide behind. With much rehearsal, you could make it look to the audience like the actors are being eaten, even though they are really behind the wolf and the bed. Perhaps they could even duck behind a curtain.

Another possibility would be for the director to work with the lighting designer on this blocking problem instead of with the set designer. Perhaps there could be a blackout when the wolf eats Grandma and Little Red Riding Hood. They could run offstage while the lights are off, and when the lights come up, the wolf could pat his stomach and look full.

There are always different ways to block a play, and no two directors block exactly alike.

In the musical *Miss Saigon* lighting and sound are used as a helicopter lands on the stage.

BLACKOUT

Stage Picture Freeze Dance

You may already be familiar with freeze dance. If so, here's a new twist on an old favorite.

Props
●●●●●●
Radio, record player, tape deck, or CD player

 Freeze dance is when one person plays music while everyone else dances. When the player turns off the music, everyone must freeze. If the player can see you move, you're out and must help watch for others who move when the music is turned off. When the player turns the music on again, everyone continues his or her dance until the music is once again turned off. The game continues until all but one person has been caught moving when the music is off. The last person is the winner.

In theater, it is important for the audience to always be able to see everyone onstage. If you are blocking someone so that the audience can't see him or her, if someone is blocking you, or if you have your back to the audience, that makes a poor stage picture. For a good stage picture, people in front might want to pose low to the ground so they are not blocking anyone behind them, while people in the back should strike tall poses so that they can be seen even if they are behind someone. Everyone should face the audience.

In **Stage Picture Freeze Dance**, you not only have to freeze when the music stops, but you must also be sure to make a good stage picture. You are out if:

1. You move after the music has stopped.
2. You freeze with your back to the audience.
3. You freeze blocking someone.

Continue the game until one person is left.

The actors in the musical *Starlight Express* perform on roller skates.

Musical Characters

The characters found in musical theater are often larger than life; that is, they use big gestures and facial expressions.

Rooster in *Annie* and the Witch in *Into the Woods* are two examples of villainous characters in musical theater. Tim Curry played Rooster in the 1982 movie version of *Annie*. He wore a dark mustache and dark ratty clothes in order to appear evil sneer. He used his eyebrows to make his eyes look evil, and his lips made an evil sneer. It was easy to believe that his character hated little girls and was extremely greedy.

Bernadette Peters played the Witch in the Broadway production of *Into the Woods*. She wore the typical black witch dress and pointy hat, complete with long green fingernails. She used her fingers to gesture in scary ways, casting spells and warning others of her power. She talked in a screechy, witchy voice and laughed an evil laugh.

Coincidentally, Bernadette Peters also played Rooster's girlfriend in the movie version of *Annie*, so she is no stranger to villain roles in musicals.

The leading young character in a musical is called an *ingenue*. Julie Andrews has played numerous ingenue roles in musicals, including *The Sound of Music*, *My Fair Lady*, and *Camelot*. Her characters are often young women who fall in love with the leading man. Julie Andrews's sweet voice, proper posture, and kind facial expressions help to create these believable characters.

The comic relief or larger-than-life character in musicals is called a *character role*. They are often smaller parts than the ingenue or villain, but they are fun to play because they make the audience laugh the most. The role of the dentist in *Little Shop of Horrors* may not be big (he sings only one song) but Steve Martin was happy to play the role in the movie version because it's fun to play a crazy dentist who enjoys drilling people's teeth. And some female actors would much rather play the mean yet funny stepsisters who get to liven things up in *Cinderella*, instead of the leading role who must play it straight.

There are, however, a number of character actors who have found leading roles that suit them perfectly. Carol Channing and Ethel Merman are known for a loud, gruff singing voice—not what you'd want for most leading ladies, but perfect for Dolly Levi in *Hello Dolly*. Barbra Streisand played the unusual leading role of the star of the Ziegfeld Follies, Fanny Brice, in *Funny Girl*.

Tale Mime

To practice the gestures and expressions of the characters in a musical, try this game of pantomime. In pantomime you cannot speak, so you must use your body and face to communicate to the audience or other players. As you pantomime a famous moment from a fairy tale, the other players guess the name of the fairy tale.

 Think of a famous scene in a fairy tale, such as Gretal pushing the witch into the oven. Try acting it out without speaking. Be sure to show the emotions on your face. For example, Gretal might look scared at first, then strong and brave, then triumphant because she has conquered the witch. The witch might look mean at first, then scared as she is pushed into the oven. After you have rehearsed your pantomime scene, show it to the other players and see if they can guess what scene you are performing.

Ideas for Tale Mime Scenes

✦ The prince trying the glass slipper on Cinderella

✦ The witch giving Show White a poison apple

✦ The prince climbing up Rapunzel's hair

✦ Sleeping Beauty pricking her finger on a spinning wheel

✦ Little Red Riding Hood discovering that her

✦ Grandma is really the wolf

✦ Goldilocks trying out each of the three bears' chairs

✦ The wolf trying to blow down the brick house

Encore! Encore!

Play *Nursery Mime*. The musical *Babes in Toyland* has a lot of nursery-rhyme characters. Little Boy Blue and Little Bo Peep are characters who help save Toyland from the evil villain.

Try to pantomime nursery rhymes instead of fairy tales. Here are some ideas for nursery rhymes to act out without speaking.

✦ Jack and Jill climbing up the hill and falling

✦ Little Miss Muffet eating her curds and whey and seeing the spider

✦ Old King Cole calling for his pipe, bowl, and fiddlers three

✦ Little Bo Peep looking for her sheep

✦ Old Mother Hubbard finding no bone in her cupboard

Play **Show Mime**. If you are working on a play, try a run-through without speaking. Pantomime your way through the entire play. See how it makes you use your body and face. Next time you run the show while speaking, try to use the same big gestures and expressions.

During the curtain call the actors gesture to the orchestra, conductor, and/or accompanist so the audience knows to applaud for them as well.

Joker's Wild

In a musical, characters are often exaggerated. For example, you probably will never meet a live person quite as bossy as Lucy in *You're a Good Man, Charlie Brown*. The character is exaggerated so that she is bossier than people in real life. One way that a director might ask the actors to become bigger or more exaggerated is to tell them to "intensify" what they are doing. This game helps you come up with ideas on how to intensify or exaggerate your character's traits. You decide how to act based on what card you draw.

Props
••••••
Deck of cards

 Choose a word that describes you. For example, you might choose the word fun. Think of a scale from 1 to 10, and imagine that 5 is in the middle, or of average intensity. Imagine, for example, someone who is a 5 when it comes to fun. They are sometimes fun, and sometimes not. Now imagine someone who is a 1 when it comes to fun. They never have any fun. They are the opposite of fun. Next, imagine someone who is a 10, or the most intense.

They are so much fun that all they can do is have fun. They might have so much fun that they're crazy.

Choose one player to be the dealer. The dealer calls out the number 1, and everyone walks around as someone who is a 1 of his or her word. For example, the person who is a 1 in fun might walk slowly and never smile. Next the dealer calls out 2, and the players walk and move as if they are a 2 of their word, so they might be a little more fun, but not much. The dealer calls out each number in order up to 10. See how it changes the way everyone moves. When the number 5 is called out, everyone might look normal, but by the time you reach 10 things might look a bit silly. Next, have the dealer call out numbers, not in order. He might say 7, then 3, then 9. Practice this until everyone has played each number a couple of times.

Next, take a deck of cards and remove all of the jacks, queens, and kings. Leave in the jokers and aces. The dealer holds the cards facedown for the players to choose one. Don't show anyone else your card. Pick a partner and decide on a scene to act out or improvise. Take turns acting and being the audience. When you are acting, act like someone who is the number that you drew for the word that you've chosen to act out. For example, if you drew the number 6, act like someone who is just a little above average when it comes to fun. An ace counts as a 1 in this game. The jokers are wild, so if you draw one of the jokers, you can pick any number you like. Remember that your partner is also acting like her number, so don't be surprised if she acts strange. After you have acted out a short scene, let the audience guess what number you drew.

Encore! Encore!

If you are working on a play, choose a word that describes your character to play this game, and act out scenes from your play with the number you draw.

Frank Sinatra and Marlon Brando played gambling men in the movie version of the musical *Guys and Dolls.*

Programs, Programs, Get Your Programs Here

A *program* is the booklet or paper that the audience receives as they enter the theater. It contains information about the play that they are going to see. If you decide to create a program for your play, there are a number of things you may want to include.

Title Page

The title page usually looks like this:

You're a Good Man, Charlie Brown

Program

Emanon Theater Company
(name of the theater)

presents

You're A Good Man, Charlie Brown
(name of play)

Directed by
(name of director)

Choreographed by
(name of choreographer)

Musical direction by
(name of musical director)

Actors often perform eight shows a week. Monday is the *dark night*, or night off, with two matinees (afternoon shows) during the week.

Cast Page

The cast page lists each of the characters and the actors who play them. It will often say "In order of appearance," meaning the first character to speak is listed first, and so on.

Here's an example.

```
Schroeder . . . . . . . . . . Josh Andrews
Linus . . . . . . . . . . . . Marty Smith
Lucy . . . . . . . . . . . . Rachel Gold
Patty . . . . . . . . . . . . Hali Berg
Snoopy . . . . . . . . . . Ian Goodman
Charlie Brown . . . . . . . Danny Shultz
```

Understudies may also be listed on this page.

Synopsis of Scenes

For some plays it is helpful for the audience to know the setting and time period of each scene. Here's an example.

```
Scene I
Time: Summer 1982
Place: The beach
```

If there is an intermission, it may be listed on this page, too. Here's an example.

> *"There will be a 10-minute intermission."*

If not, the program may say:

> *"This play is performed without an intermission."*

Musical Numbers

In many musicals, the songs are listed in order, along with the characters who sing each song. Here are some examples.

> *"You're a Good Man, Charlie Brown"*—Ensemble
>
> *"Suppertime"*—Snoopy

Director's or Author's Notes

Sometimes the director or author writes a page about their concept for the play, or some background information that might help the audience understand the play.

Bios

Bio is short for biography. A bio is a short paragraph that tells about the past experiences of the actors and staff members. For example, an actor will include plays she has performed in, sometimes including the roles that she has played. (The **Write a Bio** activity will help you write a bio for yourself.)

Staff

Here the staff is listed with their jobs followed by their names, just like in the cast list. There is often a staff list for the play and a staff list for the theater. The staff list for the play may include the following:

Director
(the person who casts and stages the play)

Assistant director
(the person who helps with the casting and staging of the play)

Choreographer
(the person who stages the dances)

Dance captain
(the person who leads dance rehearsals)

Musical director
(the person who teaches the music to the actors and works it into the play)

Set designer
(the person who designs the background and scenery)

Costume designer
(the person who designs what the actors wear)

Lighting designer
(the person who designs the lighting effects)

Sound designer
(the person who designs the sound effects)

Props master
(the person responsible for objects carried onstage by actors)

Stage manager
(the person who runs rehearsals with the director, and then runs the technical aspects of the play during the performances from the light booth)

Assistant stage manager
(the person who helps run rehearsals and shows)

Stage crew
(the people who change the scenery)

Light board operator
(the person who runs the light board, bringing the lights up and down during the play)

Sound operator
(the person who runs the sound during the play)

The staff list for the theater may include the following:

Managing director or producer
(the person in charge of the business elements of the theater)

Artistic director
(the person in charge of the artistic elements of the theater)

Marketing director
(the person in charge of the flyers and advertisements for the play)

Outreach coordinator
(the person who helps people come see the play who might not otherwise have a chance to do so)

Publicist
(the person who tells newspapers and other media about the play)

Box office manager
(the person in charge of the tickets for the play)

Photographer
(the person who takes photos of the play)

Acknowledgments

Here the theater can thank people who helped with the show, or who donated items or money to the show or the theater company. Many theater companies are not-for-profit. This means any profit a play makes goes back into the theater, not to the producer. Not-for-profit theaters are tax-exempt. When they buy things they don't have to pay taxes on them. Also, they have a board of directors who is responsible for raising funds for the theater. The members of the board of directors are listed on the acknowledgment page, as well as any foundations, corporations, or individuals that gave grants or contributions to the company. If an actor's mom donated an old dress for the play, for example, she would be acknowledged on this page.

Rules

Going to a play is different than going to a movie because the actors are right there, live and onstage. They can hear the audience, and it can affect how they perform. Some programs list rules to remind the audience to be polite. Here are some examples.

> ◆ Do not enter or exit during the performance.
>
> ◆ No eating or drinking in the theater.
>
> ◆ Please turn off beepers and cellular phones.
>
> ◆ No flash photos.
>
> ◆ Do not talk during the performance.

Ads

To help raise money for your play, you can sell advertising space (ads) in your program. Ads can be for businesses, or they can be special notes to cast members from their friends and families. For example, a business ad might read:

> *Eat at Judy's Restaurant*
> *Located right around the corner from the theater.*
> *Free dessert with this ad.*

A personal ad might read:

> *Hali, you're a terrific Patty!*
> *We love you!*
> *Love, Mom and Dad*

If you have another play coming up you can advertise it here, too.

Write a Bio

For your program, or as a getting-to-know-you exercise for a group of actors, write a bio for yourself. Here are steps you can follow to create your own biography.

Props

Pen

Paper

 Write down your name, the character you are playing, your age, grade, and the name of your school.

Name	Lisa Winters
Character	Marian
Age	13
Grade	Freshman
School	Niles High School

Next, make a list of any plays you have been in, what characters you played, and the name of the theater, school, or other location where it was performed. Include school plays, plays at your church or temple, even plays you've acted out with your friends at home. (It's OK if you have never been in a play before. You can skip ahead to the next part.)

The Electric Sunshine Man, court clerk, Devonshire School

Fiddler on the Roof, dancer, Community Center

Cinderella, the Queen, Community Center

Man of LaMancha, horse, Niles High School

Now list your hobbies.

Singing, dancing, basketball, aerobics, coin collectng

Write down where you live, and who you live with.

Where	*Skokie, Illinois*
Who	*Mom, Dad, brother Martin, dog Sam*

Finally, put it all together in paragraph form.

Lisa Winters (Marian) is a 13-year-old freshman at Niles High School. She has performed as the court clerk in *The Electric Sunshine Man* at Devonshire

School, as a dancer in *Fiddler on the Roof*, and the Queen in *Cinderella* at the Community Center, and as a horse in *Man of LaMancha* at Niles High School. Her hobbies include singing, dancing, playing basketball, aerobics, and collecting coins. She lives in Skokie, Illinois, with her mom, dad, her brother Martin, and her dog Sam.

If this is your first play, you could replace the second sentence with:

She is pleased to be making her theatrical debut with this play.

After everyone has written a bio, read them out loud to each other.

Veronica Asbury

You can make up a stage name for yourself by using your middle name as your first name and the street you live on as your last name. Usually it works; for example, doesn't "Veronica Asbury" sound elegant? Sometimes, however, it doesn't work, like with "Mary Eleventh Street."

Curtain Call Game

A t the end of a play, the actors take their bows. This is called a curtain call. Even actors whose characters have died in the play take a bow. It's a way for the audience to honor the actors and let them know how much they appreciated their performance.

Often in productions of *Little Shop of Horrors*, two people will come out to bow whom the audience has not seen before. This is the voice of Audrey Two and the person who moved the puppet of Audrey Two. Audrey Two is the name of the plant, and it usually takes one actor to play its voice from offstage and another to be inside the puppet making it move.

As a general rule, the curtain call is for actors only. Directors, designers, producers, and crew don't bow.

An actor's bow can be a stiff bow from the waste down, or a deep curtsy. There are many different ways to do it. Play this game to practice for your curtain call. Take your bow any way you like, and the other players will repeat what you do.

Everyone lines up in the back of the room facing the front. If you are in a theater, line up in the last row of the audience seats. The first person runs to the front of the room, or center stage, and takes a bow, however they like. It can even be silly. For example, you could jump around and say, "Hey nonny nonny and whoopde doopde do" with a bow at the end. Whatever you do, the rest of the players must imitate you exactly from where they are in the back of the room. Then they applaud and cheer loudly as you run back to the end of the line, and the next person goes. Continue until everyone has had at least one turn.

Actors come onstage, sometimes individually and sometimes as a group, and then join hands and bow following the lead of the middle-most person in the line of actors.

5

I Got Rhythm

Musicals are full of toe-tapping, knee-slapping, finger-snapping music, and you can be, too. Anyone can be a musician and everyone can sing. Even if you think you can't carry a tune, you can still learn to speak in rhythm. In *The Music Man*, the character of Professor Harold Hill talk-sings his most famous song, "Trouble." *Talk-sing* means talking in rhythm to the music. When Frederick Loewe and Alan J. Lerner found out that Rex Harrison, the actor they wanted for the lead role in *My Fair Lady*, couldn't sing on key, they purposely created songs that he could talk-sing just for him.

If you don't think of yourself as a singer or a musician, perhaps you are a songwriter. Many songwriters have written for musical theater. Even the rock-and-roll band *The Who* wrote music for a musical called *Tommy*.

Some of the games in this chapter are for singing, some are for rhythm, some are to help you make up new songs, some are for breath support, and some are to learn more about instruments and the orchestra that plays in a musical.

The term "orchestra pit" refers to where the band or orchestra plays in a theater. It is called a *pit* because it is traditionally located below the audience in front of the stage.

Musical Styles

Musical writer Oscar Hammerstein said, "A musical can be anything it wants to be. There is only one thing a musical absolutely must have—music." Different musicals have different kinds of music. In *Grease*, the music is rock and roll. In *West Side Story*, the music is jazz. There are opera musicals and even country-and-western musicals.

In the musical *Working*, different songwriters wrote the music so the styles would vary. For example, the mill worker sings a folk song about the hardships of working in a factory, while the valet-parking attendant sings a jazzy number about the fun of driving other people's cars.

Try this game to explore different musical styles, and see what style you like best for your musical. If you are creating your own musical, you can use this game to make up new versions of songs to use in your show.

 As you sing a song, another player calls out different styles. Sing in the style called out and see how it changes your song.

Choose a song everyone knows, such as "Do-Re-Mi" from *The Sound of Music*. Try singing it in different musical styles. Here are some ideas.

Two or more players

+ Rock and roll
+ Jazz
+ Opera
+ Rap
+ Blues
+ Country and Western
+ Lullaby
+ Heavy Metal
+ Folk
+ Disco

See if others can guess what style you are singing.

Encore! Encore!

 For a fun challenge, have one or more players start singing. After a few lines, another player (one who is not singing) calls out a musical style, such as opera. Without stopping, the singers continue the song as if it were an opera. After a few more lines the caller names a new style, such as blues. Each time a new style is called, the singers change their style of singing, but keep the song going. The singers continue until the song comes to an end.

The Jazz Age was from 1920 to 1929. Many jazz musicals were written during this time.

Use or Become Instruments

The orchestra plays an important part in a musical, and each instrument in the orchestra is needed to make just the right sound. In this game, explore how a musician plays her instrument and the way the instrument sounds. You can become either the instrument or the musician and create a symphony with the other players.

 Choose one player to be the caller. Everyone else walks around the room. When the caller names an instrument, everyone quickly finds a partner and begins creating music. One partner is the musician and the other is the instrument. As the musician "plays" the instrument, the instrument makes music, or hums in a way that sounds like the instrument.

Don't plan in advance who your partner will be or who will be the musician and who will be the instrument. Just take the first partner you see, and somehow work together without talking. Continue making music until the caller makes a "cut" signal with her hands. Then walk around the room again until the next instrument is called. Be sure to call instruments from all areas of the orchestra.

Here are some ideas.

✦ Woodwinds	*Clarinet, Flute*
✦ Strings	*Violin, Bass*
✦ Brass	*Tuba, Trombone*
✦ Percussion	*Snare Drum, Triangle, Cymbals*

Encore! Encore!

Instead of making the sounds of the instrument, choose a short song such as "Row, Row, Row Your Boat" or "Twinkle Twinkle Little Star" that everyone plays together when the instrument is called.

Composer George Gershwin was born in Brooklyn, New York, in 1898. His parents wanted his older brother Ira to take piano lessons, but George convinced them that he wanted to play piano more. The two brothers worked together on a number of musicals—George writing the music and Ira the lyrics. One of their most famous songs was also the title of one of their most famous musicals, *Strike up the Band*.

Catch Phrase

Many plays have a catch phrase, or an important phrase sung over and over. In *The Phantom of the Opera*, the phrase, "The Phantom of the Opera is here!" is repeated. In *Evita*, the title is sung over and over. In *Working*, the longer phrase, "Hey, somebody, don't you want to hear the story of my life?" often starts a character's story.

In this game you will explore what your character is all about. You choose a catch phrase that your character would say and act out a scene saying only that phrase.

Choose a phrase. If you are working on a play, choose a phrase that your character might say. For example, in *You're A Good Man, Charlie Brown*, Linus might say, "I love my blanket," and Lucy might say, "You're a blockhead." Practice saying your phrase many different ways. Try it loud, then soft. Try it fast, then slow. Try saying it with different emotions such as happy, sad, scared, or excited. Try putting an emphasis on different syllables. For example, Linus could say, "**I** love my blanket," meaning you don't love it, I do. Or he may say, "I **love** my blanket," meaning I certainly don't hate it. He also could say, "I love **my** blanket," meaning mine, and not yours. Or he could say, "I love my **blanket**," meaning my blanket, not my pillow. After you have said your catch phrase many different ways, try singing it.

Choose a partner, and decide on an action your characters could be doing together, such as painting a fence. Begin acting out a musical scene, singing only your catch phrase. You can sing it all different ways: Loud, soft, fast, slow, angry, happy, and many other ways to communicate with your partner. Remember that you can only sing that one phrase. Try to let your scene partner know what you want without breaking the singing-only-the-one-phrase rule, and see how far the scene goes just by singing that one phrase.

Andrew Lloyd Webber was only 21 years old when he composed the music for *Jesus Christ Superstar*.

Someone's Day

Many songs in musicals tell a story about a character. In *Once Upon a Mattress*, the play opens with the minstrel singing the story of the *Princess and the Pea*. In *Working*, the teacher sings about her day in the classroom. In this game you will make up a song about the day someone has had.

Interview someone and ask her about her day. Find out what she ate, where she went, and who she saw. For example, your interview might go like this.

Q: *What's your name?*

A: *Barbara.*

Q: *What did you have for lunch?*

A: *Macaroni and cheese.*

Q: *Where did you go today?*

A: *To the store.*

Q: *Who did you see?*

A: *I went with my mom, and I saw my friend, Charlie.*

Q: *Did you do anything else?*

A: *I came home and did my homework.*

Next choose a style of music, such as blues. Then make up a blues song about Barbara's day. You don't have to write it down, just improvise. There is no wrong way to do it; anything you sing is OK.

Composer Irving Berlin's real name was Israel Baline.

For example, Barbara's blues song might go like this.

Barbara is a girl who eats macaroni and cheese.

Barbara is a girl who eats macaroni and cheese.

She likes to shop with her mom,
and she always says "please."

Barbara saw her friend Charlie at the store.

I said, Barbara saw her friend Charlie at the store.

But she had to go home and do her homework,
what a chore.

Finish your song by repeating a catch phrase about Barbara, such as:

She's got the homework blues.

She's got the homework blues!

Encore! Encore!

Try **Someone's Day** in a performance setting. Ask a member of the audience to tell you about his day, then take a suggestion from the audience for the style of music. See if the entire cast can create a song together. It's challenging because you really have to listen to each other and go along with what everyone else is singing. See if you can improvise a catch phrase together for the end.

Song Jams

There are many songs in musicals that have more than one person singing many different parts. In *Fiddler on the Roof*, the song "Tradition" starts with each of the family members singing about what they do: the papas, the mamas, the brothers, and the sisters. At the end of the song all of them sing their parts at the same time, creating harmony. In *You're a Good Man, Charlie Brown,* four book reports become four-part harmony as Charlie Brown, Lucy, Linus, and Schroeder all sing about their book reports on the *Tale of Peter Rabbit*. In *Guys and Dolls*, three different gamblers sing about different racehorses in three-part harmony.

A *jam session* is when musicians get together to play music without planning in advance what the songs will be or what instruments will be used. They just choose songs everyone knows and play along however they want. In this game you will create a jam session by singing different parts of a song everyone knows.

Props
••••••
A drum will add to this game, but is not necessary

 Choose a song everyone knows, such as "Row, Row, Row Your Boat." Everyone sits in a circle. One person can play the drum to keep the rhythm. Start singing the song over and over, but not every part. Choose certain parts to sing, and play around with the words. For example, some people may repeat, "Merrily, merrily, merrily, merrily" while others may sing, "Row, row, row" and still others will sing, "Life is but a dream." You can change the melody, the notes that you sing, the rhythm, or the speed and emphasis you use when you sing the words,

 but keep the tempo (time of the overall beat) the same so that everyone is together. Listen to what others are doing so you sound good together. You can change the song's words, too. You can sing, "Merrily stream, merrily dream" or whatever comes to mind.

Keep the jam going for a long time and see how it changes. Sometimes it may be loud, and other times soft. At some point the song should come to a natural end.

Row, row, row

Merrily, merrily, merrily, merrily

Life is but a dream.

You may not recognize the name Harold Arlen, but you know his songs. He wrote "Somewhere Over the Rainbow" and the other songs from *The Wizard of Oz.*

Encore! Encore!

If you are working on a musical, choose a song from the play for a song jam. Here are some examples of songs from plays that work well for this game.

✦ "Do-Re-Mi" from The Sound of Music

✦ "You're Never Fully Dressed Without a Smile" from Annie

✦ "Oklahoma" from Oklahoma

✦ "Follow the Yellow Brick Road" from The Wizard of Oz

Mrs. Sadie

In musical theater actors must project, which means to speak loudly so everyone in a large theater can hear you. In order to do this, actors use good breath support. *Breath support* is deep breathing from the diaphragm so that an actor doesn't strain her voice. Here's an exercise to help you practice and improve your breath support.

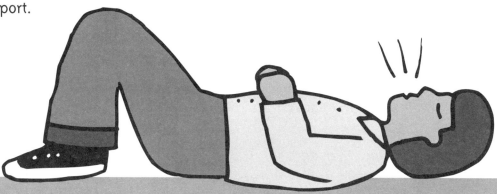

 Take a deep breath and see what happens to your body. If your shoulders rise or your stomach sucks in, you are not breathing in the best way to support your voice. Below your chest and above your stomach is your diaphragm. When you breathe, your diaphragm should expand. Put your hands there and see if you can feel it getting bigger when you take a deep breath. Then let the breath outand feel it getting smaller. If it is difficult to feel, try laying down on your back with your knees bent and your feet on the floor.

When you have practiced breathing using your diaphragm, try this song to help improve your breath support. Make up a tune to sing this song.

The words are:

Mrs. Sadie

She was a lady

She had a daughter

That I adored

I used to court her

I mean the daughter

Every . . .

Now take a deep breath and try repeating the days of the week three times without taking another breath.

Sunday, Monday, Tuesday, Wednesday, Thursday, Friday, Saturday

Sunday, Monday, Tuesday, Wednesday, Thursday, Friday, Saturday

Sunday, Monday, Tuesday, Wednesday, Thursday, Friday, Saturday

At half past four.

If you were able to say the days of the week all three times in one breath, sing the song again and try saying them four times. Next try five and so on. If you practice this song often, you will find that your breath support actually improves.

"No you can't!"   "Yes I can!"

In the musical *Annie Get Your Gun*, two characters argue in a song called "Anything You Can Do I Can Do Better."
One of the arguments they have is who can hold a musical note longer.

Act-a-Song

All musicals have a story to tell. You can make a song into a short musical by acting it out.

 Try acting out the children's song "Little Bunny Fu Fu." First, make a list of characters. For "Little Bunny Fu Fu" you will need:

Bunny

One or more field mice

Good fairy

Chorus

Decide who will play the bunny, mouse or mice, and the good fairy. Everyone else will be the chorus.

Begin with the chorus singing:

CHORUS

Little Bunny Fu Fu
Hopping through the forest
Scooping up the field mice
And bopping them on the head

While the chorus is singing, the actors playing the bunny and the field mice act it out. First, the actor playing the bunny hops around. Then he finds the mice and bops them on the head. (Remember, you are only acting, so don't really bop the other actors on the head. Just pretend.)

Then the chorus continues the song:

CHORUS

Down came the good fairy, and she said

GOOD FAIRY

(singing)
Little Bunny Fu Fu
I don't want to see you
Scooping up the field mice
And bopping them on the head

GOOD FAIRY

(talking)
I'll give you three chances.
If you don't stop, I'll turn you into a goon!

CHORUS

But the next day . . .

The chorus sings from the beginning and all the actors continue from the beginning. This is repeated three times. After the last time:

GOOD FAIRY

(talking)
Little Bunny Fu Fu
I gave you three chances.
Now, you're a goon!
(She waves her magic wand, and the actor playing the bunny makes a goon face.)

CHORUS

Hare today, goon tomorrow!
Curtain

See if you can think of other songs that tell stories that would be fun to act out. Here are some ideas.

✦ "The Bear Song" (You know, "The other day, I saw a bear . . .")

✦ "Mary Had a Little Lamb"

✦ "Splish Splash I Was Taking a Bath"

✦ "Three Little Monkeys Jumping on the Bed"

✦ "The Purple People Eater"

On an episode of the television show *Ally McBeal*, a lawyer used the song "Trouble" from *The Music Man* as a closing argument in a courtroom trial.

Lip Sync

In *Singing in the Rain*, there is a character whose voice is so annoying that someone else has to sing for her. The singer stands behind the curtain and sings into a microphone that the audience cannot see, while the character pretends to sing into a microphone in front of the curtain. She moves her lips and even her hands and face to appear as if she is singing. This is called *lip syncing*.

 Choose a partner and think of a song you both know, such as "The Itsy Bitsy Spider." Then decide who will be the singer and who will lip-sync. The singer should go behind a curtain, or just behind an open door where she cannot be seen. The lip syncer should stand in front of the audience. When the singer begins to sing, the lip syncer pretends to sing, moving her mouth and doing the hand movements for the song. See how close you can come to making it look like the lip syncer is actually singing.

There's a very funny part in *Singing in the Rain* when the voice gets faster and slower as she sings, and the lip syncer, or person trying to mouth the words, has a hard time keeping up. When the lip syncer doesn't keep up, it looks funny because the words don't match the lips.

As you try this game, the singer should vary her pace. Try singing the song very fast and see if the lip sycner can keep up with the hand movements at the same time as she tries to mouth the words. Then have the singer get very slow, like a video going in slow motion. Have the singer go back and forth from fast to slow while the lip syncer tries to keep up.

 In the Broadway production of *South Pacific*, Mary Martin actually washed her hair onstage as she sang "I'm Gonna Wash that Man Right Out of My Hair."

Concentration

This warm-up game is said in rhythm. Players must think quickly and keep the rhythm going as they name items from different categories.

 Sit cross-legged in a circle. Choose one player to select the first category, but don't say it out loud yet. Begin making a rhythm by slapping each hand on one leg at the same time, clapping once, then snapping with the right hand, then snapping with the left hand. Repeat this over and over until everyone is used to the rhythm.

Next, say the following as you keep the rhythm:

> Concentration
> Now in session
> Thinking of
> Names of _____
> Beginning with

Oak

When you get to the blank, the player chosen to pick the first category says out loud the category he has picked.

After saying, "Beginning with," the player who chose the category starts by saying something in that category. The game continues clockwise, each player saying an item in the chosen category in rhythm. To keep the rhythm, always say your item as you slap your legs.

Rules

1. Don't repeat an item that someone else has said.

2. Don't pause or go out of rhythm.

3. When a rule is broken, the player who broke it is out of the game. She stays in the circle, but does not clap, snap, or name an item. Continue the game until there is only one player left.

Here is how the beginning goes with the rhythm:

Con	slap your legs
Cen	clap your hands
Tra	snap right
Tion	snap left
Now	slap your legs
In	clap your hands
Ses	snap right
Sion	snap left
Thinking	slap your legs
Of	clap your hands
(pause)	snap right
(pause)	snap left
Names	slap your legs
Of	clap your hands
(pause)	snap right
(pause)	snap left

(Chosen category, such as:)

Trees	slap your legs
(pause)	clap your hands
(pause)	snap right
(pause)	snap left

Beginning	slap your legs
With	clap your hands
(pause)	snap right
(pause)	snap left
Oak	slap your legs
(pause)	clap your hands
(pause)	snap right
(pause)	snap left
Red	slap your legs
Wood	clap your hands
(pause)	snap right
(pause)	snap left

Continue until someone is out.

♪ *Every person who is still in the game keeps the rhythm throughout the entire game, even when it is not his or her turn to speak.*

Here are some ideas for other categories.

✦ Titles of plays

✦ States

✦ Cities

✦ Countries

✦ Girls' names

✦ Boys' names

✦ Movies

✦ Television shows

✦ Fruit

✦ Vegetables

✦ Desserts

✦ Presidents

Broccoli!

Emily!

In *Oliver*, the song "Food, Glorious Food" lists different kinds of food. In *Joseph and the Amazing Technicolor Dreamcoat*, the song "Joseph's Coat" lists the colors found in Joseph's coat. In the song "Book Report" from *You're a Good Man, Charlie Brown*, Lucy sings a list of different vegetables.

Avocado

Here's a rhythm and clapping game that uses big words for practicing your diction. *Diction* is the art of pronouncing words clearly.

Four players stand in a tight square, facing in. Player one is across from and facing player three, and player two is across from and facing player four.

The hand movements go like this:

1. Clap your own hands once.

2. Clap the hands of the person across from you once. Players one and three clap their hands above, while players two and four clap their hands below.

3. Clap your own hands once.

4. Clap the hands of the person across from you once. Players two and four clap their hands above, while players one and three clap their hands below (the opposite of step 2).

5. Clap your own hands once.

6. Clap the hands of the person next to you once. Players one and two turn and clap each other's hands, and players three and four turn and clap each other's hands.

7. Clap your own hands once.

8. Clap the hands of the other person next to you once. Players one and four turn and clap each other's hands, and players two and three turn and clap each other's hands.

9. Repeat, getting faster for as long as you can as you recite the following saying:

> *Avocado is the name of the game,*
>
> *If you miss it, you must have a word to say.*

Repeat the saying over and over with the hand movements. Get faster and faster until someone misses a clap or looses the rhythm. When that happens, the person who lost the rhythm must think of another word to say instead of avocado. Four-syllable words work best. Start over with the new word, such as Mississippi:

Mississippi is the name of the game,

If you miss it, you must have a word to say.

Repeat it with the claps, faster and faster, until the rhythm is lost again and a new word is chosen.

Here are some suggestions for four-syllable words.

- ✦ Macaroni
- ✦ Locomotive
- ✦ California
- ✦ Alexander
- ✦ Pizzeria
- ✦ Arizona

Avocado

Mississippi

Gershwin's musical *Girl Crazy* was renamed *Crazy for You*, and did much better with its new name than it had before.

Telephone Song

In the musical *Bye Bye Birdie*, telephone calls between teenagers become a showstopping song as they each sing their parts in different phone calls with one another. Here is a phone call song that will help you learn each other's names and warm up your singing voices.

 Decide on one player to go first. He will be the first name you say. Use the following script and speak in rhythm.

ALL
(sing to the first person)
Hey, _____ (first person's name, such as Corey)!

COREY
Someone's calling my name.

ALL
Hey, Corey!

COREY
I think I hear it again.

ALL
You're wanted on the telephone.

COREY
If it's not _____ (Corey fills in the blank here with another player's name) Jamie, I'm not home.

ALL
(sing to Jamie)
Hey, Jamie.

JAMIE
Someone's calling my name.

ALL
Hey, Jamie.

JAMIE
I think I hear it again.

ALL
You're wanted on the telephone.

JAMIE
If it's not Gary, I'm not home.

Everyone now sings to Gary.
Continue until all players have had a turn.

Bye Bye Birdie, the first musical that used the rhythms of rock and roll, won the Tony award for best play in 1966.

Shay Shay Coolay

In the song "I Won't Grow Up" from *Peter Pan*, Peter Pan sings lines from the song and the lost boys repeat after him. This theater warm-up also works as a call and response game. It warms up your voice with tongue-twisting words that are fun to say, and it warms up your body as you repeat the movements of the leader. It's also a great listening game, and teaches the concept of *give and take*, a very important tool on stage. When the leader sings, everyone gives focus to the leader. When the group sings, they take the focus and sing out loud. They then give the focus back to the leader for the next line.

 Stand in a circle and choose one player to go first. He goes into the middle of the circle and becomes the song leader. He sings the song one line at a time and makes gestures and movements to go along with it. The rest of the players repeat whatever movements he makes.

This song is thought to be from an African folk song, but the words have changed a bit. They are spelled phonetically here.

SONG LEADER

Shay shay coolay.

GROUP

Shay shay coolay.

SONG LEADER

Shay cofisa.

GROUP

Shay cofisa.

SONG LEADER

Cofisa longa.

GROUP

Cofisa longa.

SONG LEADER

Cha cha chee longa.

GROUP

Cha cha chee longa.

SONG LEADER

Hey. Ooo.
  (pause)
Hey hey hey. Milay lay.

GROUP

Ooo.
(pause)
Milay lay.

Next, choose another player to be the leader and lead with all new movements.

Ali Baba and the Forty Thieves

In **Shay Shay Coolay** you repeat the words after the leader. In this game you speak at the same time as the leader, but you repeat the leader's movements.

 Sit in a circle and choose one player to be the leader. Throughout the game, everyone repeats this phrase in rhythm:

Ali Baba and the 40 thieves

While everyone is saying this, the leader makes hand movements. For example, he might clap 7 times the first time it is said. Without pausing, the group then claps their hands 7 times while saying, "Ali Baba and the 40 thieves." At the same time the group is clapping, the leader is doing something else with his hands, such as snapping his fingers. The other players repeat

this action while still saying, "Ali Baba and the 40 thieves." The leader does something else while the players are snapping their fingers, such as patting his head. Continue the game for a few minutes and then let someone else be the leader.

This game is tricky because you have to watch the leader and remember what he does, at the same time as you are performing his previous movement.

In the musical *Oliver*, a group of pickpockets is led by a character called the Artful Dodger.

Make a Musical Shaker

You can use a musical shaker to help keep time with the rhythm in your games and songs. You can also use the shaker to accompany a dance.

Props

Construction paper

Scissors

Markers or crayons

Toilet-paper roll

Tape

Beans, macaroni, seeds, or popcorn kernels

Cut out two circles from the construction paper. Each circle should be about the size of the palm of your hand. Use the markers to decorate one side of each of the circles. Decorate your toilet-paper roll with the markers, too.

Tape one circle over one end of the toilet-paper roll. Use a lot of tape so it is on there tight and will not come off.

Place some beans, macaroni, seeds, or popcorn ker- nels into the roll. Hold it with the closed end on the bot- tom so they do not fall out. You don't need a lot, just enough to make a good shaking sound. Tape the other circle of construction paper to the other end of the toi- let-paper roll. Again, use a lot of tape.

Use your shaker along with your songs, and make up ways to dance with it!

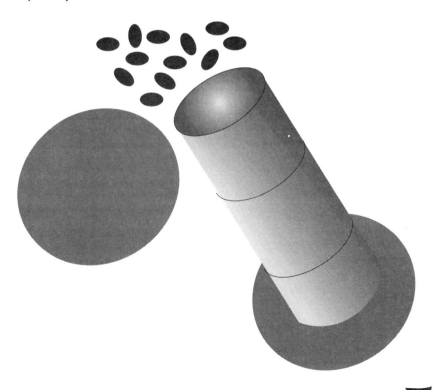

Encore! Encore!

Fill different shakers with different ingredients. See if others can tell a shaker filled with macaroni from a shaker filled with seeds. See what different sounds they make.

You can make a rain stick by using a wrapping-paper roll instead of a toilet-paper roll. You can use your rain stick for the game **Talking Stick** in "Musical Reviews."

The music for *Fiddler on the Roof* was inspired by a kind of folk music called klezmer. Similar to polka, klezmer music is festive and usually upbeat with string instruments and woodwinds. It originated in Poland, Romania, Russia, and the Ukraine. American jazz music has influenced today's klezmer bands.

6

Gotta Dance

Musical theater has some of its roots in classical ballet. Just as a ballet tells a story through dance and music, a musical tells a story through dance, music, singing, and dialogue.

Dancers use their bodies to show how they are feeling. They make shapes with their bodies to show what kind of character they are, and they move with their bodies in a rhythmic way to show action.

You can find all kinds of dancing in musicals, but tap dance and jazz dance are among the most common.

A Chorus Line is a musical about dancers auditioning for a role in the dance chorus of a Broadway musical. One of the songs, "At the Ballet," tells about three of the dancers' experiences in ballet class, and what made them want to be dancers when they grew up.

The activities in this chapter will give you some ideas for creating dances and will help you practice your own dance techniques.

Dance Shapes

Dancers use their bodies in many different shapes as they dance. This activity will help you practice different dance shapes.

 See how many different shapes you can make with your body. Try each of these.

✦ Small and round like a ball

✦ Wide as can be, including your toes and fingers

✦ Tall and proud

✦ Crouched like a fierce lion

Choose a shape you like and move around, keeping the shape. Try moving fast, then slow. Listen to different music and see how this changes your shape or the way you move.

After you have practiced different shapes, get into a group of three and decide who will start with which of the following shapes:

✦ Small and round

✦ Crouched or wide

✦ Tall and outstretched

Begin dancing, but be sure to watch each other. You may change shapes, but there must always be one of each shape. If the player who was small and round decides to stretch and grow very tall, the player who was tall and outstretched must change her shape. Continue the dance until each player has been each shape a few times.

Irving Berlin's song, "Alexander's Ragtime Band," started a ragtime dance craze.

Story Dance

In a musical, a story is told to the audience with the help of music and dance. The movements of the dance help the audience to understand the story and also make it fun to watch. This game will help you come up with ideas to add movement to your musical. As you make up a story, you make up movements for it, too.

Stand in a circle. Pick someone to begin. She makes up the first sentence of a story. It can be about anything. She also does a movement for every word of her sentence. The movement can illustrate the word; for example, for the word bird you can flap your arms as if they are wings. Or the movement can be just for fun, such as jumps, hops, or waves. After the first person says her sentence with movements, everyone repeats the sentence with the movement. The second person in the circle says the next sentence, continuing where the first person left off. The second person adds his own movement to every word in his sentence. The group repeats both sentences in order with movement. The third person adds on, and the group repeats the entire story. Continue until everyone has at least one turn and you have a complete short-story dance.

Here's an example of how this game might work.

MICHAELA

A little mouse found a coin in a garden.

Michaela's movements to each word are:

Word	Movement
A	clap
Little	squeeze fingers together
Mouse	make whiskers on face
Found	one hand over eyes
A	other hand over eyes
Coin	arm circle over head
In	one hand on hip
A	other hand on hip
Garden	spin around

Then everyone repeats the sentence with movement.

PAUL

The coin was shiny and new.

Paul's movements to each word are:

The	*one arm makes a muscle*
Coin	*the other arm makes a muscle*
Was	*arms straight down at side*
Shiny	*jumping jack*
And	*arms straight out*
New	*kick*

Now everyone repeats Michaela's sentence with movements and follows this with Paul's sentence with movements.

MEGAN

She tried to take it home.

Megan's movements to each word are:

She	*arm circle*
Tried	*hands on head*
To	*hands on knees*
Take	*wiggle body*
It	*bend down*
Home	*jump up*

Everyone repeats all three sentences, in order, with movements.

GREG

But it was too heavy.

Greg's movements to each word are:

But	*hands on ears*
It	*tilt head to one side*
Was	*tilt head to other side*
Too	*wiggle fingers*
Heavy	*fall down*

Finally, everyone repeats all four sentences, in order, with movements.

If you are creating an original musical or variety show, you may want to write down the story you have just made up, along with the movements. It will make a good dance number in your show.

Fred Astaire's real name was Frederick Austerlitz. He was born May 10, 1899, and found his famous dance partner, Ginger Rogers, in 1933.

Rhythm Names

This game is great for learning each other's names. It also shows how everyone's name has a rhythm, and how to make up a song and dance for your group.

 Stand in a circle and choose one player to go first. She says her name out loud and claps on each syllable. Everyone repeats her name, with the clapping, eight times in rhythm. Then the next person does the same, and so on, until everyone has had a turn. Listen to how different names make different rhythms. Next, have two people stand in the middle of the circle. Try saying and clapping their names together, such as Sophie, Alexander. Repeat that rhythm eight times as you march around them.

The next part of the game will take some memory skills. This time, when Sophie says her name, she will make up a movement, such as twisting her body. Then, when Alexander goes next, he must say Sophie's name first, do her movement, and then say his own name and do his own movement. The next person to go says Sophie's name and does her movement, Alexander's name and his movement, and then adds his own name with a unique movement. Continue adding on until the last person must remember everyone's names and movements.

Now that everyone has a unique movement that goes with his or her name, make up a song that includes everyone's name in it. When you sing a name, do the movement for that name. Here's a song where you can add in any names and make up your own tune or use one that's familiar to everyone, like "Twinkle, Twinkle Little Star."

> *I like Sophie, I like Andy, I like Alexander, I like Jake.*
>
> *I like Molly, one two three.*
>
> *I like Colby and they all like me.*

...and they all like me!

There is a Russian version of *My Fair Lady* called *Mya Prekrasnaja Lady*.

Shake to Maloo

Many dances in musicals call for different ways to walk, dance, and move your body. In *The Music Man*, there is a marching song called "Seventy-Six Trombones," and in *The Wizard of Oz* the actors often skip in the song "We're Off to See the Wizard."

 You can try many different ways to walk, dance, and move in this song, sung to the tune of "Skip, Skip, Skip to Maloo." As you sing it, shake your body and make up your own shaking dance.

Shake, shake, shake to maloo.

Shake, shake, shake to maloo.

Shake, shake, shake to maloo.

Shake to maloo my darling.

Replace the word shake with other words and change your dance. Here are some ideas.

- ✦ Twist
- ✦ Bounce
- ✦ Hop
- ✦ Jump
- ✦ Nod
- ✦ Flap
- ✦ Kick
- ✦ Boogie
- ✦ Drum
- ✦ Stomp
- ✦ March
- ✦ Clap

If you are playing with a group, take turns choosing the word and play follow the leader, letting the person who chose the word lead.

> *The Music Man* won the Tony Award for best musical in 1958, beating out *West Side Story*.

Happy Feet

Many musicals have tap dancing in them. Tommy Tune is a famous dancer and choreographer. He has tap-danced in many musicals, including *My One and Only*. Some people think that when he tap-dances it looks like his feet are happy. Play this game and see if you can make your feet dance with different emotions.

Choose one player to be the caller. The caller puts on some music and everyone else dances, using his or her feet to hop, skip, jump, and step to the music. The caller calls out an emotion for your feet. She might say "sad feet." See if you can dance like your feet are sad. Next, she might call out "excited feet." See how that changes your dance. Other things she might call out include:

- ✦ Scared feet
- ✦ Happy feet
- ✦ Shy feet
- ✦ Hungry feet
- ✦ Silly feet
- ✦ Serious feet

After you have tried many kinds of feet, you can add on by having the caller call out different kinds of arms, too. See if you can do two different ones at once, such as "shy feet and silly arms" or "scared feet and happy arms."

Encore! Encore!

After you have danced with different kinds of feet and arms, have the caller choose one set, such as "Hungry feet and sad arms." Let everyone dance like that for a moment. Then the caller calls out "switch," and everyone must immediately dance with sad feet and hungry arms. Then she calls out "switch" again, and you must switch back. See what a funny dance you can create this way.

The musical *Candide* calls for a lot of different kinds of dancing, including waltzes and tangos. In *Peter Pan*, Captain Hook calls for a kind of dance called a tarantella, and Peter does a soft-shoe dance as he sings the song "Wendy."

Jokey Hokey Pokey

One or more players

You probably know how to do the Hokey Pokey, but you have probably never done the **Jokey Hokey Pokey**. The song is the same, but the parts of the body are what make this dance so crazy and so much fun.

 Stand in a circle and choose one player to go first. He yells out "Jokey Hokey Pokey" and an unusual body part, such as eyelashes. Everyone does the Hokey Pokey with his or her eyelashes like this:

You put your eyelashes in.
(Move your head toward the middle of the circle and bat your eyelashes.)

You put your eyelashes out.
(Move your head out of the circle.)

You put your eyelashes in.
(Move your head into the circle.)

And you shake them all about.
(Bat your eyelashes very quickly.)

You do the Jokey Hokey Pokey
And you turn yourself about.
(Put your arms up, shake your hands, and turn around in a circle.)

That's what it's all about.
(Clap three times.)

Continue around the circle until everyone has said "Jokey Hokey Pokey" and a body part.

Some ideas for unusual body parts for the **Jokey Hokey Pokey** are:

- ✦ Thumb
- ✦ Big toe
- ✦ Kneecap
- ✦ Hair
- ✦ Heel
- ✦ Nose
- ✦ Tummy
- ✦ Lips
- ✦ Chin
- ✦ Tongue
- ✦ Heart
- ✦ Earlobe

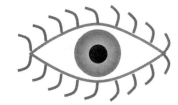 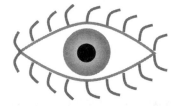

The hand jive is a dance done with only the hands by the characters in the musical *Grease*.

Contact Dance

A dancer will often lead with a part of his body, then change which part he is leading with as the dance changes. In this game see how it feels to dance leading with different parts of your body.

Props
Music

Choose a partner and decide who will be the dancer and who will be the contact person. Turn on the music and have the contact person tap the dancer somewhere on her body, such as her shoulder. The dancer should begin to dance, leading with that shoulder. It doesn't matter how she dances, as long as the shoulder leads the rest of her body in her movements. After a moment, the contact person should tap her somewhere else, such as her head. The dancer continues her dance, but she now leads with her head. The contact person should continue to tap her in different places. The taps can come faster and faster. See how the dancer moves and changes with each tap. After you have danced for a while, switch so that the contact person is now the dancer and the dancer is the contact person.

Some things to remember with this exercise:

✦ You must be able to trust your partner and know that he will tap you lightly and not in a way that can hurt. Talk about this trust before you begin.

✦ Remember to breathe, and keep breathing throughout the game. Imagine your breath going through the part of the body you are leading with.

✦ Try not to think too hard about how the dance looks. Just follow your body, and the dance will be beautiful.

The musical *I Do, I Do* has only two characters in it. It's about the relationship between a husband and wife.

Group Mirrors

Here is an idea for choreographing a ballad or slow song. One player leads while the others mirror her movements.

Props

Slow music

Make a good stage picture (see **Stage Picture Freeze Dance** in "A Performer Prepares") and choose a player who everyone can see to be the leader. Everyone (including the leader) should be facing the audience; so, the leader will have to be downstage, or closest to the audience, in order for everyone to be able to see her.

Begin the music. The leader makes slow movements, and everyone does what she does. The movements should flow smoothly together so that it is easy for everyone to follow along. The movements should be so slow and smooth, and the others should follow so closely, that the audience should not be able to tell that someone is leading. The movements also have to be big, such as long arm circles or leans, so that everyone onstage can easily see what the movements are.

After you have practiced moving together, try this exercise with feeling and energy. Think about the mood of the music, and imagine that you are giving the energy of the music to the audience with every move.

 Pas de deux is a ballet term for when two dancers dance together.

Object Dance

In *Annie*, the characters dance around with mops and buckets in the song "Hard Knock Life." In *You're a Good Man, Charlie Brown*, Linus does a soft-shoe dance with his blanket, and Snoopy dances with his supper dish. In *Fiddler on the Roof*, there is a dance where the men have to balance a bottle on their heads while they dance. And in *Singing in the Rain*, Gene Kelly does a famous dance with an umbrella as he sings the title song. Dancing with different objects is a fun way to show what your character likes (such as Linus with his blanket), or to make up unusual dance numbers.

Props
......

A variety of objects to dance with

Music

 Give everyone an object and turn on some music. Have everyone dance around with their object. Try dancing like you love the object, then like you hate it. See how it changes your dance.

Try adding object dances to a story, such as *The Three Little Pigs*.

Here's the cast list to act out *The Three Little Pigs* with object dances:

Narrator

First pig

Second pig

Third pig

Wolf

And the following objects:

Straw

Sticks

Bricks (made from construction paper or a light material such as papier-mâché)

Scarves, ribbons, or other objects for a wind dance

NARRATOR

Once upon a time there were three little pigs. They decided it was time to build their own houses. The first little pig built his house out of straw.

(The first little pig does a straw dance.)

The second little pig built his house out of sticks.

(The second little pig does a stick dance.)

The third little pig was the smartest. He built his house out of bricks.

(The third little pig does a brick dance.)

NARRATOR

One day the big bad wolf came to the first pig's house and said . . .

WOLF

Little pig, little pig, let me in!

FIRST PIG

Not by the hair on my chinny chin chin.

WOLF

Then I'll huff, and I'll puff, and I'll blow your house down!

(Wolf does wind dance as he huffs and puffs.)

NARRATOR

The wolf blew down the house, and the first pig ran to his brother's stick house. The wolf followed.

WOLF

Little pigs, little pigs, let me in!

FIRST AND SECOND PIG

Not by the hair on our chinny chin chins.

WOLF

Then I'll huff, and I'll puff, and I'll blow your house down!

(Wolf does wind dance as he huffs and puffs.)

NARRATOR

The wolf blew down the second house, and the two pigs ran to their brother's brick house. The wolf followed.

WOLF

Little pigs, little pigs, let me in!

PIGS

Not by the hair on our chinny chin chins.

WOLF

Then I'll huff, and I'll puff, and I'll blow your house down!

(Wolf does wind dance as he huffs and puffs.)

NARRATOR

The brick house was too strong, and the wolf couldn't blow it down. He decided to climb down the chimney, but the pigs quickly built a fire and put a pot in the fireplace. The wolf fell into the pot, jumped up, and ran away howling. The first and second pigs decided to build brick houses just like their brother.

(All three pigs do a brick dance.)

If you have a larger cast, try having a chorus of dancers play the houses and do object dances as the wolf blows them down.

Here are some ideas for objects you can partner with in your dances.

- ◆ Scarves
- ◆ Balls
- ◆ Brooms
- ◆ Hula hoops

- ◆ Umbrellas
- ◆ Fans
- ◆ Feather dusters
- ◆ Ribbons

- ◆ Bells
- ◆ Maracas
- ◆ Tambourines
- ◆ Teddy bears

There is a sword dance in the musical! *Brigadoon* about a magical land that only appears once every hundred years.

Interpretive Dance

Interpretive dance is a dance that tells a story. Many African dances contain moves that might remind you of planting seeds or gathering vegetables because the dances originally told a story about the harvest. Some Chinese dances tell stories of swans or even of drinking tea.

Create your own interpretive dance. Here are two ideas for your interpretive dance.

Butterfly Dance

Props
● ● ● ● ● ●

Music that reminds you of a butterfly

Scarf, if you wish

 Begin your dance as a caterpillar. Crawl and slink to the music as a caterpillar would. Imagine the movements of a caterpillar and make a dance out of them.

Next, dance like a caterpillar building his cocoon. If you have a scarf, use the scarf in your dance. As you dance, wrap the scarf around you like a cocoon.

Then, slowly begin to awaken and emerge from the cocoon as a beautiful butterfly. Use the scarf as your wings as you discover what you have become. Fly for the first time. Fly to the music. See how it feels to be a brand-new butterfly. Perform your interpretive dance for others and see if they can tell what it's about.

Tree Dance

Props
● ● ● ● ● ●

Music that reminds you of trees

 Begin your tree dance as a seed planted in the ground. Slowly grow with the music. Sprout branches and stretch out as the tree's branches grow bigger and bigger. Imagine the tree through the seasons, beginning with winter. Dance like a tree in the cold wind. Shiver and shake as the winter gets colder. Next comes spring. Your dance can become more calm as leaves begin to grow. Let your hands open and bloom. In the summer, birds may come to nest and children may play on you. See how you can dance to show these things. Finally, in the fall, the wind returns and your leaves blow around. Now change your dance so that you are no longer the tree; instead, you are a leaf. Blow in the wind, harder and harder, until you fall off of your tree. Float, float, float to the ground for the end of your dance.

Encore! Encore!
Try this interpretive dance with a partner. One of you act as the tree and the other as a leaf. See how you can dance together.

Here are some other ideas for interpretive dances.

- ✦ A thunderstorm
- ✦ An egg hatching
- ✦ A flower blooming
- ✦ Guppies becoming frogs
- ✦ An egg frying
- ✦ A baby bird learning to fly
- ✦ A popcorn kernel popping
- ✦ Clothes in a washer or dryer

The story of the *Titanic* has been made into a musical, but it's not the first musical that takes place aboard a ship. Cole Porter's *Anything Goes* takes place aboard a luxury cruise ship on its way from New York to London.

Dream Sequence

Some musicals have dream sequences, or songs and dances that happen in a character's dream. In *Fiddler on the Roof*, Tevya tells his wife about a nightmare he had where the ghost of his mother-in-law tells him who his daughter should marry. As he tells her the dream, the chorus acts it out. In *Oklahoma*, a dream sequence consists of a dance that foretells of danger for Curly, the main character.

Dream sequences can be different than the rest of the play because dreams can be so much stranger than real life. To show that it is a dream, the characters in these scenes might move slower than in the rest of the play. The lighting might be dimmer or different colors. The music might sound scary or warped, or if it is a good dream, happy and magical.

Props
. . . . . .
Music that reminds you of a dream

 Make up a dream sequence. You can create your own story line with a dream, or take one from classic literature. When you are getting to know your character, it is important to think about what he dreams of—what his hopes and fears are. This is a great character development game for all roles,

even if you do not want a dream sequence in your final production.

Here are some ideas of stories that could have a dream sequence.

- ✦ Rip Van Winkle might dream as he sleeps for 20 years.

- ✦ In Aesop's fable *The Tortoise and the Hare*, the hare takes a nap in the middle of the race because he is so sure he is going to win. Imagine what he is dreaming about.

- ✦ Perhaps the wolf has time for a nap after eating Grandma, while lying in bed waiting for Little Red Riding Hood to appear.

- ✦ Cinderella might dream of the ball before or after she attends it.

Once you chose a dream to portray, choose music that goes with your character's dream. For example, the hare may dream of winning the race, so he may dance to music fit for a champion. The wolf's music might be slow and scary, and Cinderella's music might be lively and upbeat. Remember that anything can happen in a dream. The hare might dance with giant trophies. The wolf might do a tango with Little Red Riding Hood. Cinderella might dream of her stepsisters waiting on her for a change. Try to show what your character is dreaming through movements.

The title song from the musical *Oklahoma* is now the state song of the state of Oklahoma.

Make Dancing Wings

Here's how to make your own dancing wings. Choose colors that go along with your dance or character. For example, butterfly wings might be bright and multicolored, while you would use all white for swans. Wear a matching colored leotard and tights to complete the costume.

Props

Scarf-like material, such as chiffon or a light polyester

Ruler

Scissors

Elastic

Pen

Needle

Thread (for a performance-quality costume) or

Safety pins (for short-term fun)

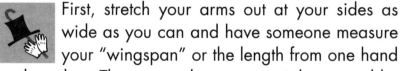 First, stretch your arms out at your sides as wide as you can and have someone measure your "wingspan" or the length from one hand to the other. Then spread your material on a table.

Measure and cut out a piece as long as your wingspan. Fold your material in half to find the center of the top edge. This will be where your neck goes.

Lightly wrap the elastic around your neck, mark this place, and then cut the elastic an inch or two larger than this mark. Sew the ends of the elastic together so you have a circle of elastic. Wrap a little of the neck area of the fabric around ¾ of the elastic circle. Sew where the material and elastic touch to secure.

Cut two pieces of elastic, each a little longer than all the way around your wrists. Sew the elastic wrist circles to each end of the top part of the material at either end. These will be where your hands go.

Place the middle elastic over your head and pull down so that the elastic band fits around your neck. Pull one arm through each of the elastic wrist circles. Try dancing like a bird and see how your wings flow as you fly around.

♫ *If the elastic is uncomfortable around your neck, sew some fabric around the elastic like a hair scrunchie.*

Encore! Encore!

For short-term fun, you can safety pin the material to the neck and sleeves of your shirt, instead of sewing it.

A *pirouette* is a dance move where the dancer spins around on one leg.

7

An Actor's Life for Me

Actors of all ages use games to help improve their acting. Some games, such as **Have You Ever** and **Categories**, help actors learn more about theater. **Have You Ever** is a good physical warm-up as well.

In order to focus and get ready for rehearsal, actors often play games like **When I Talk, You Answer** and **Amoeba**.

Working together with other actors is an important part of being in a play. Games like **Trust Me, Cops and Spies**, and **How High Can You Go?** are great games for doing this.

Improv is an important skill for all actors. It is also a playwriting tool. If you are creating an original musical or play, you can improvise scenes and then write down what you liked from each improvisation. **The Bowl Game** is a great improv warm-up because you talk without planning in advance what you will say. **Who Stole the Cookies?**, **Channel Surfing**, and **Munchkins** are a few improv games that could lead to actual scenes for an audience.

Remember, when playing theater games, the most important rule is to have fun.

Have You Ever

Because it requires some running around, this game is used to warm up your body. It is also good for getting to know each other and for learning about theater. One player says something they've done before in theater, and everyone else who has done it also races for a place in the circle.

Props

Chairs—one less than there are people playing

Have everyone sit in chairs in a big circle with one person standing in the middle. The person in the middle asks a question about theater that begins with "have you ever . . . ?" It should be something that the person in the middle has done. Everyone else who has done this must immediately get out of his or her seat and run to another empty seat. While they are doing this, the person who asked the question must also run to an empty seat. Whoever was not able to get to an empty seat is now in the middle and must ask a "have you ever" theater question.

Five or more players

Here are some ideas for "have you ever" questions.

- ◆ Have you ever forgotten your lines?
- ◆ Have you ever seen a play on Broadway?
- ◆ Have you ever been backstage?
- ◆ Have you ever acted like an animal?
- ◆ Have you ever worn stage makeup?
- ◆ Have you ever put on a puppet show?
- ◆ Have you ever made a mask?
- ◆ Have you ever played an instrument?
- ◆ Have you ever tap-danced?

Encore! Encore!

Play **Pantomime Have You Ever**. This time, the questions don't have to be about theater; they can be anything that you can act out without using words or sounds. The person in the middle says, "Have you ever . . ." and then begins to pantomime (act out an action without words) an activity that she has done, such as playing baseball. The others begin to guess what she is doing by shouting out their answers. As soon as someone shouts out the correct answer, the person in the middle yells, "Go!"and everyone who has done it runs to another chair. Here are some ideas for "have you ever" questions to pantomime.

+ Have you ever baked cookies?

+ Have you ever raked leaves?
+ Have you ever gone fishing?
+ Have you ever put on lipstick?
+ Have you ever washed a dog?
+ Have you ever braided your hair?
+ Have you ever planted a seed?

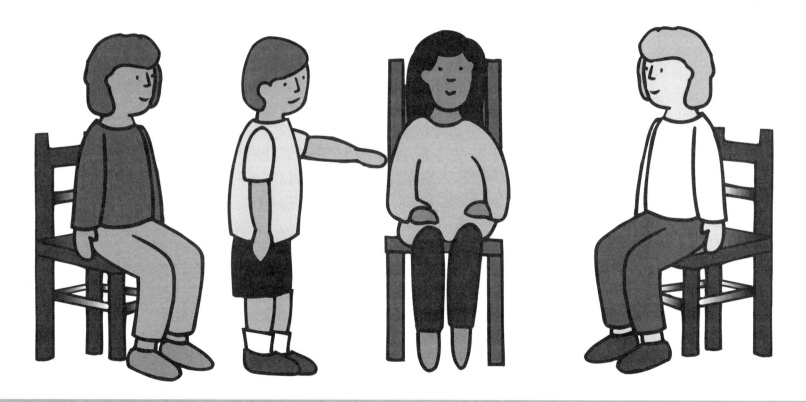

The term "Broadway" doesn't just refer to the actual street. The district actually goes from 40th Street to 50th Street, and from 7th Avenue to 8th Avenue.

Categories

In this game you have to think of theater things that start with different letters of the alphabet. You get points if no one else thought of the same thing(s) you did.

Props

Pens

Paper

 Each player begins with a piece of paper and pen. Begin by turning the paper sideways so that it is horizontal to you. Fold the paper in half from left to right, so that the paper now looks like a program, and then fold that in half again. Now you've made four creases and four equal-size columns.

In the first part, write numbers one through five, going down. This is where you will write your categories. Now think of five categories that have to do with musical theater. Different people should choose the categories.

Here are some category ideas.

- ✦ Names of plays
- ✦ Songs
- ✦ Types of dances
- ✦ Styles of music
- ✦ Musical instruments
- ✦ Famous actors
- ✦ Character names
- ✦ Costume pieces (things you wear)
- ✦ Things found backstage in a theater
- ✦ Items found in a makeup kit
- ✦ Set pieces (furniture used in a play)
- ✦ Sound effects

Next to each number, write in a selected category. All players should have the same category next to the same number. Here's an example.

1. Names of plays

2. Musical instruments

3. Costume pieces

4. Items in a makeup kit

5. Sound effects

One person, who is chosen to be the leader, asks one player to silently say the alphabet until the leader says "stop." (If the chosen player reaches the end of the alphabet before the leader says stop, he or she should start again.) When the leader says "stop," the chosen player says the letter they were on out loud so all the other players hear. Everyone writes this letter at the top of the second section of their paper. They then quickly write something in each category that begins with that letter. For example, if the letter is R, your page might look like this:

R

1. Names of plays   Rent

2. Musical instruments   Reed

3. Costume pieces   Raincoat

4. Items in a makeup kit   Rouge

5. Sound effects   Roar

As soon as one person has filled in something for each category, they say "stop" and all the other players stop writing. If you didn't get something in each category, it's OK to leave it blank.

The person who said "stop" reads her first answer out loud (the name of a play in this example) and, in turn, everyone else reads his or her answer for that category. If someone else said the same thing as the person who said "stop," then you do not get a point. But if no one else said it, you do get a point. Continue down the list and keep track of your points.

Sometimes in this game there are disagreements. For example, players may not want to count "reed" as a musical instrument. It is a type of instrument, but not a specific instrument. When this happens, everyone votes thumbs up or thumbs down on whether or not to accept this answer. The majority rules.

After all categories have been read, count up your points and write the number next to the letter R. The leader begins round two by once again having someone say the alphabet in his or her head and then when the leader says stop, the chosen player says the letter they were on out loud. Everyone writes this letter at the top of their third box and round two begins.

For example, if the letter was P your page might look like this:

	R - 3	**P**
1. Names of plays	Rent	Peter Pan
2. Musical instruments	Reed	Pipe organ
3. Costume pieces	Raincoat	Pants
4. Items in a makeup kit	Rouge	Pancake base
5. Sound effects	Roar	

In this round you may not have had time to finish before someone said "stop," so number five is left blank. Again, the person who said "stop" begins and everyone reads what he or she has written one category at a time.

If no one else said *Peter Pan* for names of plays, you would get two points in that category because both Peter and Pan begin with the letter P.

You may not get points for the same word twice in one round, so you could not have said "pan" for a sound effect in addition to *Peter Pan*.

Play one last round and add up all of your points for all three rounds. The person with the most points is the winner.

Stop!

On Broadway it costs about $8,500 to rent a theater for one day.

When I Talk, You Answer

This is a focus warm-up, and can even include singing and dancing if you wish. One player will be your voice, and you'll be the voice for another player.

 Choose one person to be the director. Everyone else stands in a circle. The director goes around the circle saying, "When I talk to you (points to someone), you answer (points to the person on the first person's left)." Everyone speaks for the person standing to their right, and the person on their left speaks for them. Then, the director begins talking to people. If you accidentally speak when the director speaks to you (instead of letting the person on your left do the talking), you're out of the game. To show that you're out, stand with your arms crossed. When you are out, the person on your left talks for the person on your right. After a few people have gotten out, start a new round. This time, the person to your left answers for you but the person to your right moves for you. The game continues until a few more people are out.

Encore! Encore!

To make this game even more challenging, skip a person so that you answer for the person two people away from you instead of right next to you.

Rodgers and Hammerstein's musical *Carousel* was based on a book called *Lilliom* by Ferenc Molnar. At first he didn't want his book to be made into a musical, but then he saw *Oklahoma* and liked it so much that he agreed to let Rodgers and Hammerstein do it.

Amoeba

In theater it is important for all of the performers to work together. Everyone has the same goal—to put on the best show they can. Therefore, a good group of actors knows that they must put all differences aside and help each other in any way they can.

There are many games and exercises you can play to help build a sense of community and cooperation among performers. Amoeba really gives you a sense of working together as one because the whole group becomes an amoeba, one creature moving together.

 Begin with everyone standing together in a close group. You should be as close as shoulder to shoulder, but not uncomfortable, and you don't need to be facing in the same direction, either. Together you are an amoeba. Just stand there together without speaking and see how the amoeba begins to move. Everyone should move together, but no one should be leading. Just see what happens. If it seems to be going to the left, go with it. If it seems to be turning around, turn, but don't take over the movement and lead. Just let it happen. See if the amoeba actually goes somewhere even though no one is leading it.

Encore! Encore!

Play **Traveling Amoeba**. Wrap a string around the group and have the outer people hold on to that string. Then have the amoeba try to go on a journey or through an obstacle course. Here's an example of a possible indoor journey.

Have the amoeba try going upstairs, downstairs, through small doorways, in an elevator, or around a sharp corner.

Here's an example of a possible outdoor journey.

Have the amoeba try going around trees, through bushes, under slides, through sandboxes, and over a hill.

Here's a possible obstacle course.

Have the amoeba try moving between chairs, over tires, around mats, and under a bridge (which can be made with a broomstick on top of two chairs).

The musical *Hello Dolly* is based on a play by Thornton Wilder called *The Matchmaker*. Wilder also wrote *Our Town*.

Trust Me

In a play, the actors work very closely together in rehearsals and performances. It is important to develop trust between the actors so that they are not afraid to open up and be the best actors they can be. Actors will often spend some time during rehearsals doing trust exercises like this one. In this game you fall backwards into the other players' arms and trust that they won't let you hit the ground.

 Stand in a circle fairly close to one another. One player stands in the middle of the circle, closes her eyes, and crosses her arms. The others say, "one, two, three, trust me." The player in the middle falls backwards into other players in the circle. They catch her and gently push her back toward the center. She falls whichever way the momentum takes her. The other players are always ready to catch her and help her back up. The person in the middle should keep her feet planted and her body stiff. To do this requires trust that the others will always catch her. Be confident, stay focused, and be ready to catch her. Never let her fall. This way she will feel safe with you.

Encore! Encore!

Another trust exercise is to have everyone stand at the end of a table and link arms with someone across from them. One player stands on the table (make sure it is safe and sturdy) with her back to the rest of the group. When the group says, "one, two, three, trust me," she falls backwards and into the arms of the other group members, keeping her body straight. The other group members safely catch her.

Some musical comedies are known for romantic, happy endings; sometimes a wedding even takes place in the final scene. The play *Guys and Dolls* ends with double the happiness because it ends with a double wedding.

Cops and Spies

In theater it is very important for actors to give and take focus, especially if you are improvising in order to write your own scenes. When an actor has a line, the other actors give her focus by looking at her and listening to her. When another actor wants to speak he takes the focus by speaking loudly and clearly so that the others know to give the focus to him. This helps the audience follow the action of the play. If more than one actor was trying to get the focus at the same time, the audience wouldn't know where to look.

In this card game the group must work together to arrest the spies. But be careful or you might arrest the wrong people!

To be successful in this game, actors must listen to each other and work together. When everyone talks at once, it is difficult to get anything done. But if you give and take you will be able to hear what others think and give your own input.

Props
● ● ● ● ● ●
Deck of playing cards

Take two aces, one black king, one red king, and enough number cards for everyone who is playing to have one card each from the deck of cards. These will be the cards you use for your game. Have everyone sit in a circle and choose one player to be the dealer. The dealer shuffles the cards that were taken from the deck, then deals them out face down. Everyone looks at his or her card but does not let anyone else see it. The two people who have aces are the spies. The two people who have kings are the cops. The game is played in three rounds.

Round One
The dealer tells everyone to put his or her head down. Then she says, "Spies have eyes." Both spies look up to see who the other spy is. Then the dealer says, "heads down" again. When the spies have their heads down, the dealer says, "Let the search begin."

Everyone looks up and begins discussing who they think the spies might be. The goal is to arrest the spies, but in this round only the spies know who they are. The others may think they heard someone moving when it was time for the spies to look up, or they may think someone is acting suspicious. The players have open discussions about who to arrest. The spies also take part in these discussions, trying to get the players to arrest the wrong people. When the conversation seems to be pointing to someone in particular, the players vote on whether or not to arrest him. If the majority of the players agrees to arrest someone, that person has one chance to defend him- or herself. They improvise a reason they should not be arrested. Then the players vote again. If there is still a majority, the player is arrested and no longer in the game. If there is not a majority, the conversation continues until another player is chosen for the vote. After one player is arrested, begin round two.

Round Two

The dealer tells everyone to put their heads down again. Then she says, "Cops are tops." Both cops look up to see who the other cop is. Then the dealer says "heads down" again. When the cops have their heads down, the dealer says, "Let the search continue."

Everyone looks up and begins the discussions again. Each cop tries not to let the players arrest the other cop, so they might defend one another if someone accuses them. The play continues just like in round two until a second person is arrested. Then begin the third and final round.

Round Three

The dealer tells everyone to put their heads down again. This time she says, "Spies have eyes, but the red cop is the very top." Then the spies and the red cop (the person who holds the red king) look up and see who's who. Then the dealer says, "heads down" again. When the spies and red cop have their heads down, the dealer says, "Let's finish the search."

The game continues just as before, but in round three two people are arrested. This time the red cop knows who to arrest and must try to convince the others. But beware, because spies can pretend to be red cops, too. After two people have been arrested, everyone turns over their card to show who they were.

You were successful if both spies and no cops were arrested.

🎵 *Even if the red cop sees that the two spies have already been arrested before the third round, the game continues until two more people are arrested.*

In 1964 the title song from *Hello Dolly* beat out the Beatles' song "Hard Day's Night" to win the Grammy for best song.

How High Can You Go?

This challenging warm-up game is easy to learn but hard to play. You really have to listen, concentrate, focus, and work together in order to be successful. It's especially fun to play often and try to beat your highest score. The goal is to count as high as you can as a group. But, only one number is said at a time, no one knows the order in which you will speak, and if two people talk at once you have to start all over again.

 Lay down in a circle with your heads in the middle and close your eyes. To begin the game, any player can start the counting by saying the number "one." Any other player can say "two," and so on. The only rule is that no two players may say the same number. It may sound easy, but because there is no planned order, you never know who will say a number. Someone has to say it, but if two people say it at the same time, you have to start all over again. See how high you can go!

Irving Berlin was paid 37 cents total royalties for his lyrics to the song "Marie from Sunny Italy." He was only a teenager. Even though he received very little money, he did get his name on the cover of the sheet music, which helped forward his career.

Bowl Game

In this fast-paced game, players try to get their teams to guess what they are describing before time runs out.

Props

Pens or pencils

Paper

Bowl

 Every player takes a pen or pencil and a piece of paper. Take a few minutes to write down 10 objects, people, or places. Tear off each word, fold it, and place it in the bowl.

Divide into two teams. Decide which team will go first, and who on that team will read first. Give the bowl to the reader. She has 60 seconds to make her team say as many words in the bowl as she can. Someone from the other team keeps track of the time. When they say "go" she reaches into the bowl, takes out a piece of paper, and reads what it says to herself. She quickly describes it to her team without saying any part of the word or phrase. She keeps describing it

until someone on her team correctly identifies what is written on the paper. For example, if the paper said "Peter Rabbit" she could not say, "He's a rabbit." If she does, the other team gets the point. She could describe Peter Rabbit by saying, "He's a bunny who was in Mr. MacGreggor's garden." As soon as one of her teammates calls out "Peter Rabbit" she tosses that piece of paper aside (don't put it back in the bowl) and takes another piece of paper. She continues until the time is up. Count up all of the pieces of paper out of the bowl to see how many points the team gets.

Here are the other rules you must follow in this game.

1. It's OK to point. For example, you could say she "has the same first name as this character (pointing to someone in the room)."

2. You can only say "sounds like" if you do not actually say what it sounds like, but instead describe it. For example, if it's a mouse, you cannot say, "sounds like" or "rhymes with house." But you can say, "sounds like a place you live in" and have your team guess "house."

3. There is no passing. If you get one you don't know, do the best you can. You're stuck with it until your team guesses correctly or time runs out.

4. The paper you are working on when "time" is called goes back in the bowl. Don't tell anyone what it was.

5. Switch off teams and players until all of the pieces of paper in the bowl are used up. The team with the most points wins.

Encore! Encore!

If you want more of a challenge and a longer game, toss all of the paper back in the bowl and play a "speed round." This time each team sits in a circle. The first player takes the bowl. When the timer says "go" she looks at the first paper. But this time she can only say one word, and only to the person on her right, not to the entire team. The person next to her can only give one answer. If it is correct, the paper is put aside; if it is wrong, the paper goes back in the bowl.

For example, if the paper says "Peter Rabbit," the reader might say "bunny." If the guesser remembers that Peter Rabbit was in the first round, he may think to say "Peter Rabbit" and win points for his team.

Next, the person who just guessed takes the bowl and gives a one-word clue to the person on his right. The game continues in the circle until the time is up. Then the papers guessed correctly are counted up. This time each correct guess is worth two points.

This round is more difficult because you only get to say one word, but if you paid attention to the first round, you've already heard all of the answers before.

Encore! Encore!

Play **Bowl Game** as a getting-to-know-you game. Ask everyone to put things into the bowl that are important to him or her, or that tell about themselves.

Play a theme **Bowl Game**. You can write down your words in advance to go along with the theme of a play. Put all of the character names, catch phrases, settings, and other things that have to do with the play into the bowl before everyone else arrives.

Who Stole the Cookies?

Many plays are based on mysteries. The play *The Mousetrap* is based on a mystery by Agatha Christie, and there is even a musical about the board game called Clue. This game makes a terrific mystery scene in your play, and is a great improv game as well. You accuse another player of stealing the cookies and say that you have videotaped proof. After you describe that videotape they act it out. But look out, because you will be accused, too.

 Players stand in a line facing the audience. The player at one end of the line goes first. He accuses the player next to him of stealing the cookies. The second player denies it. The first player can ask the second player questions, then says he has videotape proving the second player wrong. He describes what is on that tape and yells "play" as he pushes a button on his imaginary remote control. The second player then steps out in front of the line and acts out what the first player said was on the videotape. This is where you can have a lot of fun because the second player must act out whatever the first player says, no matter how silly. Then the first player yells, "freeze," and the second player freezes. The first player goes up to the frozen second player and points out to the others where the evidence is. Then, the first player yells, "stop" and the second player rejoins the line, restates her innocence, and accuses the third player. This continues until all players have had a turn.

Here is a sample of play.

* *

DEBORAH

Someone has stolen the cookies, and I believe I know who it is. I think that Kyle stole the cookies.

KYLE

It's not true! I'm innocent!

DEBORAH

Oh, really? So, I suppose you don't even like cookies.

KYLE

That's right, I don't.

DEBORAH

Then why do I have a videotape of you singing a love song to the cookie jar? Play!

(DEBORAH pushes the button on her imaginary remote control. KYLE steps out in front and sings to an imaginary cookie jar until he hears DEBORAH say, "freeze.")

DEBORAH

Freeze!
(KYLE freezes.)
As you can see
(pointing to KYLE)
he clearly loves cookies. Stop!
(KYLE rejoins the line.)

KYLE

It wasn't me! It was Katrina!

KATRINA

Me?

KYLE

Yes, you!

KATRINA

That's impossible. I wasn't even in the house that day.

KYLE

Then why do I have a videotape of you sneaking through the kitchen like an elephant wearing roller skates? Play!
(KYLE hits his imaginary remote control. KATRINA steps out pretending to sneak around like an elephant wearing roller skates until she hears KYLE say, "freeze.")
Freeze!
(pointing to KATRINA)
So you see, she was in the house that day. Stop!
(KATRINA returns to the line and accuses the next person.)
The game continues until all players have had a turn at being accused and accusing someone.

Encore! Encore!

If you are playing this game in front of an audience, take a suggestion from an audience member for a silly crime that was committed.

Channel Surfing

If you've ever surfed the channels (or sat with a remote control in front of the television and flipped the stations around), you know that there are all sorts of different shows on at one time. In this game you get to play around with different styles of acting, and also make sure you are listening to the other players. You act out a show until someone "changes the channel." Then you become the show on the new channel.

 Choose one player to be the surfer. She holds an imaginary remote control. Two to four other players are the television. Since the game starts with the television off, the players start with their backs to the audience. When the surfer says "on" the players turn around and begin acting out a television show, commercial, newscast, or anything you might see on television. They don't plan in advance, so they have to work together quickly. If one player starts a newscast, others join in, rather than trying to change it. Even if you didn't want to act out a newscast, you still have to go along so it looks like a real television show. But don't worry, because as soon as the surfer says, "change channels" you can start the next show.

The tricky part is that you have to remember what you have done and said in your scene because the surfer can also say, "rewind," "fast-forward," or "slow motion." Whatever the surfer says, the players act out.

Here is a sample of play.

• •

Michelle, Isaac, and Adam are the players; Hope is the surfer and holds the imaginary remote control.
(Michelle, Isaac, and Adam have their backs to the audience.)

HOPE
On.

MICHELLE
(to ISAAC)
Dad! Look! My nose is broken! And it's all his fault!
(gestures to ADAM)

ISAAC
(taking on the character of the dad, while ADAM becomes the brother)
Well, let's have a look at it.

ADAM

I didn't mean to break it. We were just playing ball in the house.

HOPE

Rewind.

(Players quickly act their recent lines and movements backwards.)

Play.

(Players act the exact same scene.)

MICHELLE

(to ISAAC)

Dad! Look! My nose is broken! And it's all his fault!

(gestures to ADAM)

ISAAC

(taking on the character of the dad, while ADAM becomes the brother)

Well, let's have a look at it.

ADAM

I didn't mean to break it. We were just playing ball in the house.

HOPE

Change channels.

ISAAC

It's a great day for a ball game out here.

MICHELLE

(becomes broadcaster with ISAAC)

Sure is. And the batter is stepping up to the plate.

(ADAM becomes the batter.)

ISAAC

Here's the pitch. It's a swing and a miss.

MICHELLE

That's strike one.

HOPE

Fast-forward.

ISAAC

(very quickly)

Here's the next pitch. It's a hit!

(ADAM quickly runs the imaginary bases.)

MICHELLE

(very quickly)

Homerun! The crowd goes wild!

HOPE

Rewind.

(Players quickly act the last few lines and movements backwards.)

Slow motion forward.

ISAAC

(very slowly)

Here's the next pitch. It's a hit!

(ADAM slowly runs the imaginary bases.)

MICHELLE

(very slowly)

Homerun! The crowd goes wild!

HOPE

Stop.
(The players turn their backs to the audience to show that the scene is over.)

Television's Rosie O'Donnell played the character Rizzo in the musical *Grease* on Broadway.
She is also known for breaking into musical theater medleys on her talk show.

Munchkins

You probably already know that the Munchkins are very small people who live in Oz. If you were directing the play *The Wizard of Oz*, how would you make the Munchkins appear small? You could cast shorter actors as the Munchkins, and taller actors as Dorothy and the other characters. Another option that might be funny would be to try this game and use it for your show. In this game one player is the face, voice, and body, while another player provides the arms and legs.

Props

2 bedsheets for each pair of players (jackets or anything else to cover you up can also be used)

 Get a partner and decide who will be the face (player one), and who will be the hands and feet (player two). Player two sits behind player one, who is sitting cross-legged with her legs covered by a sheet. Player one puts her hands behind her back, and player two puts his hands through player one's armholes so that his hands look like they are hers. Then player two puts his feet around player one's waist and rests them on her covered legs so it looks like she is a very small person with strange hands and feet.

If you wish, use a second sheet to cover player two's face.

Make up a scene. You could pretend to be young children in a nursery school. Try counting. Player one speaks, but player two moves his hands and feet. They must work together. If player one says, "What comes after two?" player two might hold up three fingers. If player two begins playing with his toes, player one might start reciting "this little piggy." There are many funny things you can do using a nursery-school setting. Here are some examples.

- ✦ Sing the "I'm a Little Teapot" song with movements
- ✦ Learn to tie your shoe
- ✦ Play Patty Cake
- ✦ Play Peek-a-boo

If you decide to do the Munchkin scene this way, practice singing the "Lollypop Guild" song, and pointing Dorothy in the direction of the yellow brick road.

> **Michael Jackson played the scarecrow in the movie version of *The Wiz*.**

Make a Phantom Mask

Masks have been used in theater since ancient Greece. Comedy and tragedy masks have symbolized theater for decades. Today the half mask worn in *The Phantom of the Opera* is also a theatrical symbol.

Props

Paper plate

Scissors

Pencil

String or elastic

Decorative supplies such as markers and glitter, if you wish

 To make a phantom mask, cut your paper plate so that it covers only part of your face. The traditional phantom mask covers his eyes, goes over his nose, and down the right side of his face, but you can be creative and cover whichever parts you like.

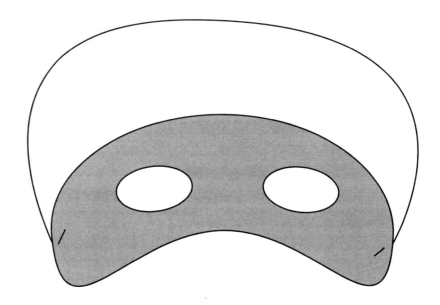

Cut out the shape you chose for your mask, but make sure that it goes from ear to ear. Hold the mask up to your face and ask someone to carefully mark where your eyes and ears are located on the mask and to make light pencil marks in these places. Cut holes for your eyes, and in both sides of the mask near where your ears are. Thread one end of the string or elastic through each ear hole and lightly knot the ends. If you used string, then you can tie your mask on behind your head. If you used elastic, gently stretch it over your head and down until your mask is in place.

The traditional phantom mask is pure white, but you can decorate yours with markers, paint, glitter, sequins, or anything you like.

In the musical *Phantom of the Opera*, a huge chandelier falls onstage.

An Actor's Life for Me

8

Show Time!

Here are a series of short plays that could be used in a performance with an American folk-hero theme. In these plays, the actors talk to the audience and sometimes get suggestions from them.

The first three plays in this chapter—*Paul Bunyan*, *Davy Crockett*, and *Sluefoot Sue*—are based on American folk heroes and would work well in a folk-hero theme show.

The scene from *Alice in Wonderland* takes place at a croquet game. This would fit into a theme show about sports. The game itself could become an object dance with mallets. There are also **Wonderland Warm-ups** in this scene.

When Emanon Theater Company of Chicago, Illinois, went looking for a theme for their show, they discovered that there are a number of children's stories that have the number three in the title. They called their show "The Triple Play." It included the short play versions of *The Three Little Pigs*, *Goldilocks and the Three Bears*, and *The Three Billy Goats Gruff* that are in this chapter. These plays were created by the cast and director through improvisation.

Paul Bunyan

Adapted by Emanon Theater Company ©1999

This play can be performed with as few as four actors playing multiple characters.

Characters

Paul

King of Sweden

Babe, the blue ox

Tim Bur

Tree

Queen of England

Sourdough Slim

Creampuff Fatty

PAUL

I'm Paul Bunyan. I'm the greatest lumberjack who ever lived, and the greatest inventor. Who invented the Grand Canyon? Me! Who invented the giant axe? Me! Who invented the cotton gin?

OTHERS (all other characters)

You?

PAUL

Well, no, actually that was Eli Whitney, but who invented the Rocky Mountains? Me!

OTHERS

No way!

PAUL

Even the King of Sweden thinks so. You see, one day the King of Sweden came to me and said:

KING OF SWEDEN

Paul, I hear you're the greatest lumberjack who ever lived.

PAUL

That's right.

KING OF SWEDEN

Well, you need to make room here in America for the Swedes coming to live here. If you can clear the land, I'll pay you.

PAUL

How much?

KING OF SWEDEN

One dollar twenty-five cents.

PAUL

Wow! You've got a deal!

So I had to log the land, which means clearing the trees in lumberjack talk. I had the help of my blue ox, Babe.

BABE

Why am I bluuuuuuue?

PAUL

Babe, you are blue because the year you were born was the year of the great blue blizzard. Blue snow fell all over. It was so deep it covered you all the way up to your eyes. Some of that blue rubbed off on you, and you became a blue ox.

BABE

Oh, thank yooooooooou!

PAUL

Now, before I could clear the trees, I needed to flatten those mountains, but I wasn't sure how. Then Babe started giving me blues clues.

 (BABE points to TIM BUR.)

So I called on my friend Big Tim Bur.

TIM BUR

What can I do for you, Paul?

PAUL

I need a hammer. But not just any old hammer. I need the biggest hammer in the entire world!

TIM BUR

I think this'll do.

 (HE pulls out a giant hammer.)

It's called MC, and you can touch it.

PAUL

Thanks! So I set to work flattening out the mountains with MC. When I was done, I even put a few streams in to look nice, and of course I chopped down all the trees to make a lot of room. Well, I actually chopped down half the trees. When I finished those, the other half looked around and laid down in fright. There was one tree that I wasn't sure was scared enough, so I axed it.

 (to TREE)

Are you scared?

TREE

Nope!

PAUL

Boo!

 (TREE falls.)

KING OF SWEDEN

Paul! I'm amazed. But I bet even you couldn't get all those logs to Sweden.

PAUL

I bet I can.

KING OF SWEDEN

Bet you can't.

PAUL

How much do you want to bet?

KING OF SWEDEN

A dollar fifty.

PAUL

You're on.
So to move all the logs out of there, I started chopping up an old river no one was using and laid it down where I needed it. I sent all the logs across the English Channel because the Queen wanted to see them, too.

QUEEN OF ENGLAND

Oh, what nice logs. Pass the tea.

PAUL

And I got them to Sweden. Pay up, Sweetie.
(KING OF SWEDEN pays PAUL.)
But I noticed something. The land I cleared was awful windy. I knew those mountains were good for something.
(OTHERS become wind.)
It was even windier than that.
(OTHERS become bigger wind.)
(to audience)
I think they need help. All of you make the wind, and blow real hard. One, two, three. Yes! That's how windy it was. I needed to make some mountains. If only I had some mole holes.
(Bell rings from offstage.)
That gave me an idea, and I called on my friend Sourdough Slim. Slim, I need you to make the best sourdough biscuits ever.

SOURDOUGH SLIM

Well, the best sourdough biscuits are healthy and good for you, so I put in a lot of healthy ingredients.
(to audience)
Raise your hand if you can think of a healthy ingredient to put in my sourdough batter.
(HE calls on audience member who suggests a healthy ingredient, such as carrots.)
Great, I'll put some carrots in. Who else has an idea for a healthy ingredient?
(HE calls on audience member who suggests a healthy ingredient, such as raisins.)
Good idea, I'll put some raisins in. Now, this dough is called sourdough. What should I put in to make it sour?
(Audience responds "lemon.")
Lemon! That's right! I'll put lemon in, and stir it all up. Here it is, Paul, what do you think?

PAUL

Well, it seems a little thin. I think we need to fatten it up.

SOURDOUGH SLIM

Better call Creampuff Fatty.

CREAMPUFF FATTY

(enters eating)
Oh, sorry, I was just eating some Bunyan rings.

PAUL

We need to fatten up this sourdough biscuit batter.

CREAMPUFF FATTY

Well, I need three real fatty things to put in this batter. Raise your hand if you can think of a fatty ingredient to put in my batter.

(Calls on audience member who suggests a fatty ingredient, such as butter.)

Great, I'll put some butter in. Who else has an idea for a fatty ingredient?

(Calls on audience member who suggests a fatty ingredient, such as chocolate.)

Good idea, I'll put some chocolate in. Now I need one more real fatty ingredient.

(Calls on audience member who suggests a fatty ingredient, such as ice cream.)

That's perfect. I'll put in some ice cream. Now, I stir it up, and there you have it.

PAUL

Now I need to take all this sourdough biscuit batter and bury it in gopher holes. Who knows what happens to biscuit batter when it sits for a while? It rises. Rises like the mercury in a thermometer.

Well, first the earth started shaking. Shaking like a go-go dancer.

(OTHERS go-go dance.)

Shaking like a chicken.

(OTHERS do the chicken dance.)

Shaking like a kid on a roller coaster.

(OTHERS act like they are on a roller coaster.)

Then the biscuits rose, and each of them formed into a mountain.

KING OF SWEDEN

These mountains are so nice, here's two dollars extra.

PAUL

Bonus! And that's how I invented the Rocky Mountains.

Curtain

Davy Crockett

Adapted by Emanon Theater Company ©1999

Characters

Davy

Panther

Cows

Book Learning Folk 1

Book Learning Folk 2

DAVY

My name is Davy Crockett and I'd like to tell you my tale. You see, one night a comet came racing to the earth. It was so big and so bright that folks thought the sun was falling.

OTHERS (all other characters)

The sun is falling! The sun is falling! We'd better tell the king!

DAVY

It wasn't the sun. It was a comet flying faster than a popcorn kernel in the microwave. When it hit the earth it made a huge bang, and suddenly I appeared. I was so big, I had a tortoise shell for a cradle, and it was as comfy as an old pair of shoes. When I got older, I was walking through the forest in Tennessee when I met a panther. He and I had quite a confrontation.

PANTHER

I like the Cubs!

DAVY

Sox!

PANTHER

Cubs!

DAVY

Sox!

PANTHER

Cubs!

DAVY

We got into quite a scuffle over that one, but when the dust cleared . . .

OTHERS

Clear the dust!
  (OTHERS clear dust.)

DAVY

It was clear there was no victor . . . nor Norman nor Steven for that matter. The panther and I shook on it and became great friends. We went on our travels together, and we happened upon a cow field.

OTHERS

Moo!

DAVY

It was *udder* chaos!

OTHERS

Moo! Moo! Moo! Moo!

DAVY

I decided I should run for election to fix all this chaos. Vote for me, Davy, Davy Crockett! I can out spit, out run, out wit, out stare, out jump, out grin any opponent. Why I can grin a raccoon out of a tree!

BOOK LEARNING FOLK 1

You can what?

DAVY

I can grin a raccoon out of a tree.

BOOK LEARNING FOLK 2

(laughing)
We're book learning folk, and we happen to know that's impossible.

DAVY

I'll prove it!
So they took me to a tree with a raccoon in it, and I gave that raccoon a great big grin.
(HE grins. BOOK LEARNING FOLK laugh.)
Hm, that's not quite enough. I'd better give it my biggest grin.

(HE grins. BOOK LEARNING FOLK laugh harder.)
Hm, this has never happened before. Maybe if all of you will grin as big as you can along with me. One, two, three, grin!
(HE grins with audience. BOOK LEARNING FOLK laugh harder.)
I can't understand it!

PANTHER

Wait just a minute! That's not a raccoon in that tree; that's nothing but a twisted knot.

DAVY

Twisted as a night away.

PANTHER

There's a raccoon in that tree?

DAVY

Not!

BOOK LEARNING FOLK 1

He's right, there's no raccoon after all. There never was.

BOOK LEARNING FOLK 2

And there's no bark on that tree either.

DAVY

That's right. I grinned all the bark right off of that old tree. I proved I had the best grin around, and I won the election!

Curtain

Sluefoot Sue

Adapted by Emanon Theater Company ©1999

Characters

Sue

Pa

Ma

Twister

Coyotes

SUE

Once upon a time, a long time ago, there lived a little girl named Sue. That's me. Now I was a cute little girl, all blond curls and big eyes and a lot of energy, and right from the beginning, I seemed to march to my own drummer.

(Other characters march around drumming until SUE marches with the most unusual step.)

When I was about one year old and it was getting time for me to learn how to walk, I started looking around at all the grown-ups walking forward and backward, and forward and backward, and forward and backward. Well I sat there for a long time thinking to myself about all the things those silly folks were missing by only seeing things from one direction, so, much to my family's amazement, I stood right up and began to walk.

(OTHERS faint in amazement.)
Sideways that is.

PA

As sideways as a sidewinder.
(SUE dances sideways.)

MA

Looks like she's shuffling to some imaginary music inside her head.

PA

From now on, we should call her Sluefoot Sue.

SUE

And that's how I got my name. Now I came from a big old Southern family that loved me very much, but also had 14 other kids, and well, I was a bit of a handful.

PA

Texas is getting too small for this family. We're heading out of here.

SUE

So we loaded the family in the wagon and off we went. Well, as we were driving along I started bouncing. It's real fun to bounce. I bounced faster and faster, until I bounced right out of the wagon, and my family didn't even notice. They just kept on going. I sat for quite a spell on that dirt road when an awful storm done started to brew off in the distance. It almost sounded like an animal set to crying for his kin, so I began wailing, too. That storm became a twister, and that big old twister must have heard me wailing cause it came right on over and picked me up. I rode until it dropped me here.
  (COYOTES greet SUE.)
A family of coyotes took me in and taught me to speak coyote.
  (SUE howls.)
That's how you say "hi" in coyote.
  (SUE howls again.)

That's how you say danger in coyote.
  (SUE howls again.)
That's how you say Peter Piper picked a peck of pickled peppers in coyote. Now, I loved my coyote family very much, but after a while I decided it was time I headed somewhere new, so I needed to get the twister to come back.
  (to COYOTES)
Will you help me wail, so the twister will come back?

(COYOTES nod.)

SUE

(to audience)
Will you help, too? Everyone wail. One, two, three.
  (All wail until twister comes back and SUE hops on.)
Bye-bye coyote family! And that's how I ended up here.

Curtain

Alice in Wonderland

Here is a scene from *Alice in Wonderland* that uses the **Wonderland Warm-Ups** activity found in "A Performer Prepares."

Characters

Queen of Hearts

Alice

White Rabbit

Other Wonderland characters such as the Mad Hatter, the March Hare, and the Cheshire cat

QUEEN OF HEARTS

Welcome, everyone, to my royal, regal, and rigged croquet game. I'm so glad that you could . . .

(Looks around and realizes SHE is alone onstage.)

Hey! Where is everybody?

(OTHERS enter quickly.)

Where's my bow?

(OTHERS bow to QUEEN OF HEARTS.)

That's better. Now, as I was saying, welcome to my royal, regal, and rigged croquet game. Of course, before we play, we must do our Wonderland Warm-Ups. One, two, three.

(Wonderland characters do Wonderland Warm-Ups. ALICE tries to follow along, but does not know them. Afterward, QUEEN OF HEARTS gives her a mean look.)

White Rabbit, distribute the mallets.

WHITE RABBIT

Yes, your majesty.

(WHITE RABBIT gives everyone a mallet. HE gives a giant one to QUEEN OF HEARTS.)

QUEEN OF HEARTS

Ah, I see you saved my lucky mallet for me.

WHITE RABBIT

Yes, your majesty.

QUEEN OF HEARTS

Excellent. Well, there's only one thing missing.

WHITE RABBIT

What's that, your majesty?

QUEEN OF HEARTS

The ball!

WHITE RABBIT

Of course, your majesty.

(WHITE RABBIT puts ball center stage.)

QUEEN OF HEARTS

Let the game begin!

(Wonderland characters do all sorts of crazy things with their mallets—everything except hit the ball. ALICE observes all of this craziness until finally SHE walks right up to the ball and hits it into the goal.)

ALICE

I win!

OTHERS (all other characters)

You what?

ALICE

Win.

(OTHERS, except QUEEN OF HEARTS, gasp and run off in fear. QUEEN OF HEARTS approaches ALICE.)

QUEEN OF HEARTS

Off with your head!

ALICE

What? You can't do that. All I did was hit the ball . . .

WHITE RABBIT

(entering quickly)
Queen of Hearts?

QUEEN OF HEARTS

Yes?

WHITE RABBIT

Remember when you made those tarts?

QUEEN OF HEARTS

All on a summer's day.

WHITE RABBIT

Well, the knave of hearts, he stole those tarts.

QUEEN OF HEARTS

And took them all away? Off with his head!

WHITE RABBIT

Yes, your majesty.
(HE exits quickly.)

QUEEN OF HEARTS

Now, then, where was I? Oh, yes.
(to ALICE)
Off with your head!

WHITE RABBIT

(entering quickly)
Queen of Hearts?

QUEEN OF HEARTS

Yes.

WHITE RABBIT

I forgot where we keep the axe.

QUEEN OF HEARTS

Off with your head!

ALICE

Now, wait just a minute. You can't just go around chopping off everyone's heads. It isn't fair. You should at least give them a chance to defend themselves. I think there ought to be a trial.

QUEEN OF HEARTS

All right, you want a trial? I'll give you a trial. Yours!
(shouting as SHE exits)
Prepare for the trial!

Curtain

 In the book *Alice in Wonderland* the mallets are flamingos and the ball is a hedgehog. You can make cutout flamingos from cardboard to use in your show.

The crazy croquet game can be an **Object Dance** (see "Gotta Dance") that you choreograph. The characters can all dance around with their mallets performing all sorts of silly movements.

The Three Little Pigs

Adapted by Emanon Theater Company ©1999

In this play, the pigs sing a lot. You could make up the songs they sing by using the exercises in "I Got Rhythm." Also, the chase scenes could become choreographed dance scenes. See the chapter called "Gotta Dance" for dance ideas.

Characters

Wolf

Pig 1

Pig 2

Pig 3

WOLF

I used to be a total nerd, the runt of the wolf litter. Always picked on for being so puny and fluffy. I desperately wanted to fit in with the other slick and cool wolves. Then, one day, on accident, I discovered my one greatest talent. You see, I had bad allergies. My nose was running, my eyes were watering, and all of a sudden I let out the hugest, most horrific sneeze in the world. Blew me right over. Also blew over everything in my path. The other wolves were pretty impressed. They thought it was funny. Who knew? My allergies made me cool. I became popular. I was on top of the world. And then I met the three little pigs.

(Pigs enter singing.)

WOLF

I'm so hungry I could eat a wagon wheel. Slim pickings here in the woods. What do I want? Oh, yeah, those three little pigs live down the street, and word is out their mom is in Las Vegas and they're home alone.

PIG 2

Look, a letter from mom.
  (reading)
Having slots of fun!

PIG 3

  (reading)
Won big!

PIG 1

  (reading)
Won enough for you to build your own house. Check enclosed.
  (PIGS sing a song to celebrate.)

PIG 2

What should we build our house out of?

PIG 3

My spontaneous mathematical computations, along with my knowledge of architecture, lead me to believe that bricks would be the sturdiest and most heat efficient. We should use bricks.

PIG 2

Bricks are so square. We need something with texture, like sticks.

PIG 1

I think we should use straw. It's bright and sunny and cozy and comfy, and it reminds me of mom's hair.

PIGS 2 AND 3

Huh?

PIG 1

You know, stiff and crunchy.

PIG 2

All right, straw it is.

PIG 3

I still think bricks would be best.

PIGS 1 AND 2

Oh, hogwash!

PIG 3

Fine.
  (to audience)
House-building montage number one.
  (PIGS sing as they build their straw house.)

PIG 2

Well our house is done.

PIG 1

What do we do now?

PIG 2

I'm cold.

PIG 1

It's freezing in here.

PIG 3

Bricks would have been warmer. Here's a blanket.
  (PIGS cover themselves in the blanket.)

PIG 1

You know what we are?

PIGS 2 AND 3

What?

PIG 1

We're pigs in a blanket!
  (WOLF sees PIGS.)

WOLF

There they are.
  (Knocks on door.)

PIGS

Who is it?

WOLF

It's the wolf and I'm going to eat you, so let me in!

PIGS

The wolf!

PIG 1

What do we do?

PIG 2

Stop, drop, and roll.
  (THEY roll around until . . .)

PIG 3

No, that's for a fire.

PIG 1

What did mom say to do when a wolf is at the door?

PIG 3

I remember. We're supposed to say, "Not by the hair on our chinny chin chins."

PIGS

(to wolf)

Not by the hair on our chinny chin chins.

WOLF

All right, you little pork rinds. I'm going to sneeze and wheeze and huff and puff and blow down your stuff.

PIGS

Look out!

(WOLF blows, chase scene, PIGS escape)

PIG 1

That was scary.

PIG 3

That was close.

PIG 2

That was wild.

PIG 1

Now what do we do?

PIG 2

Sticks are stronger than straw.

PIG 3

(to audience)

House-building montage number two.

(PIGS sing as they build their stick house. When they are done, PIG 1 sees a bug go by.)

PIG 1

What was that?

PIG 3

A termite.

PIG 2

Better get some termite traps.

(WOLF knocks on the door.)

What was that?

PIG 3

A woodpecker?

PIG 1

Better get some woodpecker traps.

PIGS 2 AND 3

Woodpecker traps?

PIG 3

There are no termites or birds pecking in brick houses.

PIG 2

Sticks always get a bad rap.

PIG 1

Speaking of rap, who's that rapping at our door?

WOLF

It's the wolf, and I'm going to eat you, so let me in!

PIGS

Not by the hair on our chinny chin chins.

WOLF

Then I'm going to sneeze and wheeze and huff and puff and blow down your stuff.

PIGS

Look out!

(WOLF blows, chase scene, PIGS escape)

PIG 3

Well, well, well. Straw and sticks. What do you have to say for yourselves?

PIG 2

I think it's time to build a brick house.

PIG 3

(to audience)

House-building montage number three.

(PIGS sing as they build their brick house.)

WOLF

I'm in search of little pigs in flimsy houses. Ah, here we go.

(knocks)

PIGS

Who is it?

WOLF

It's the wolf, and I'm going to eat you, so let me in!

PIGS

Not by the hair on our chinny chin chins.

WOLF

Oh yeah? Well it's ham hocks for everyone because I'm going to sneeze and wheeze and huff and puff and blow down your stuff.

(WOLF blows, with no success.)

PIG 3

You blowhard!

PIG 2

You're just blowing hot air!

PIG 1

Your breath stinks!

(WOLF begins to cry.)

PIG 3

Look, he's crying wolf.

PIG 2

Aw, he's just a sheep in wolf's clothing.

WOLF

Stupid allergies.

PIG 1

I never noticed how soft and fluffy he is.

WOLF

All I want to do is quit sneezing all the time.

PIG 3

Maybe we could help him.

PIG 2

Let's give him some of mom's special allergy-curing potion. It'll make him stop sneezing.

PIG 3

Hey, wolf, we think our mom's special potion could help your allergies.

WOLF

Really? You'd give some to me?

PIG 1

Sure. Here you go.

(Gives WOLF the potion, WOLF drinks.)

WOLF

I feel better already. You pigs are the best! From now on, I'm a vegetarian! I'll never eat pork again.

PIGS

Yeah!

Curtain

Goldilocks and the Three Bears

Adapted by Emanon Theater Company ©1999

This play involves playing a game with your audience. The audience will fill in the blanks for some of the important parts of this story. Before you begin, ask the audience for the following:

- ✦ A color
- ✦ A type of food
- ✦ An object
- ✦ 2 adjectives (an adjective is a word that describes something)

Now you are ready to act out the play. Remember to fill in the blanks with what the audience said. The actors will have to do a little improvising, because the play will be different every time. Also, they have to pantomime the objects, because they won't know in advance what they will be.

Characters

Narrator

Papa Bear

Mama Bear

Baby Bear

Goldilocks

NARRATOR

This is the story of _____. (Change the gold in Goldilocks to the color the audience gave, such as pink.) Pinkylocks and the Three Bears. Once upon a time there were three bears.

PAPA BEAR

I'm Papa Bear.

MAMA BEAR

I'm Mama Bear.

BABY BEAR

I'm Baby Bear.

NARRATOR

They lived in a cottage in the forest. One beautiful day they were getting ready to eat some delicious _____. (Insert the food item the audience said, such as popcorn.)

MAMA BEAR

This popcorn is too hot. (If the food had been ice cream, she could have said "too cold," or anything else that might work.)

PAPA BEAR

Let's go for a walk in the woods.

BABY BEAR

Playground! Playground!

MAMA BEAR

Yes, Baby Bear, we can go to the playground.

BABY BEAR

Yeah!
(BEARS exit.)

NARRATOR

Meanwhile, Pinkylocks came wandering through the woods.

PINKYLOCKS

This forest is too big, and I am too lost. There's a cabin. I wonder if anyone's home.
(calling)
Hello! Hello!
(no answer)
Too cool!
(SHE goes in.)
This place is too empty. They hardly have the bear necessities. Let's see what there is to eat.
(SHE looks around.)
Yum! Popcorn!
(SHE tries Papa Bear's popcorn.)
Ouch! This popcorn is too hot.
(SHE tries Mama Bear's popcorn.)
Yuck! This popcorn is too cold.
(SHE tries Baby Bear's popcorn.)
Yum! This popcorn is just right.

NARRATOR

Pinkylocks ate all of Baby Bear's popcorn. Then she went into the living room and found the bears' _____.
(Insert the object the audience suggested, such as balloons.)

PINKYLOCKS

(SHE plays with Papa Bear's balloon.)
This balloon is too big.
(Or she says another sentence that makes sense with the object.)
(SHE plays with Mama Bear's balloon.)
This balloon is too small.
(SHE plays with Baby Bear's balloon.)
This balloon is just right.

NARRATOR

Pinkylocks played with Baby Bear's balloon until she popped it. (Or broke it.) Then, she went upstairs and found the Bears' beds. She tried Papa Bear's bed, but it was too _____. (Insert the first adjective given by the audience, such as sticky.)
(PINKYLOCKS pretends to be in a sticky bed.)
Then, she tried Mama Bear's bed, but it was too _____. (Insert the second adjective given by the audience, such as crazy.)
(PINKYLOCKS pretends to be in a crazy bed.)
Finally, she tried Baby Bear's bed, and it was just right. In fact, she fell right to sleep. That's when the bears came home.

BABY BEAR

I'm hungry. I can't wait to eat our popcorn.

PAPA BEAR

Hang on a minute. Someone's been eating my popcorn.

MAMA BEAR

Someone's been eating my popcorn.

BABY BEAR

Someone's been eating my popcorn, and they ate it all up!

PAPA BEAR

This looks like a job for Detective Bear.
  (HE takes out a magnifying glass.)
Walk this way.
  (HE leads them to the living room.)
Someone's been playing with my balloon.

MAMA BEAR

Someone's been playing with my balloon.

BABY BEAR

Someone's been playing with my balloon, and they popped it.

MAMA BEAR

Who could've done this?

BABY BEAR

Look!
  (HE points.)
Footprints!

PAPA BEAR

Good work, Baby Bear.
  (They go up the stairs.)
We've got to get to the top of this. Walk this way.
  (HE leads them to the bedroom.)
Someone's been sleeping in my sticky bed.

MAMA BEAR

Someone's been sleeping in my crazy bed.

BABY BEAR

My bed's all lumpy!

MAMA BEAR

Baby Bear, get back. It might be dangerous.

PAPA BEAR

It's a little girl.
  (to PINKYLOCKS)
Little girl, wake up.

PINKYLOCKS

  (still asleep)
Time for school already, mom?

PAPA BEAR

Little girl, wake up!

PINKYLOCKS

  (still asleep)
Five more minutes.

PAPA BEAR

Little girl, you don't seem to understand. I'm a bear.

MAMA BEAR

A very big bear.

BABY BEAR

I'm a baby bear.

PINKYLOCKS

(waking up)
Bears!!!!

PAPA BEAR

Little girl, why did you come to our house?

PINKYLOCKS

Well, I was too lost, and your house was right there and . . .

MAMA BEAR

Little girl, why did you eat our baby's popcorn?

PINKYLOCKS

I was too hungry, and you left it out and . . .

BABY BEAR

Little girl, why did you pop my balloon?

PINKYLOCKS

Well, it was too fun, and I hit it too hard and . . .

MAMA BEAR

Well, little girl, I think you look too delicious!
(PINKYLOCKS screams and runs away.)

BABY BEAR

Aw, I wanted to play with her.

PAPA BEAR

I'm sorry, but I'm going to have to put my paw down. Some creatures just aren't fit to be in the house.

Curtain

The Three Billy Goats Gruff

Adapted by Emanon Theater Company ©1999

In this play, the troll has a little poem he says, and each of the billy goats come back at him with poems of his or her own. You could turn the poems into songs, like in "Musical Themes."

Each of the billy goats has a special way of walking that becomes their own dance. The littlest billy goat wears clogs, and could do clog dancing. The middle billy goat wears tap shoes, and could do a tap dance. The biggest billy goat wears sandals. You could make up a summer beach dance for him to do.

Characters

Big Billy Goat

Middle Billy Goat

Little Billy Goat

Troll

BIG BILLY GOAT

The scariest thing that ever happened to me happened last spring. My brothers and I were lucky to get through the winter because we live on a mountain, and the only things to eat during the winter are snow, slush, ice, and the occasional rock. One lucky day I found a new bridge. As far as I could see the bridge led to a field of cakes, cookies, and muffins. It was Day Old Bakery Land! As we were getting all set to cross that bridge, I reminded my brothers that we were headed someplace new, and we should protect each other. If they ran into any trouble, I'd take care of it. Well, my littlest brother wanted to go first because he had the most growing to do. He went to the bridge and started over. He was wearing clogs, so he went clip-clop, clip-clop, clip-clop. Just then a troll poked his ugly head up.

TROLL

Hey, little kid, I live under here. What are you doing on my roof?

LITTLE BILLY GOAT

(dancing)

The reel. I'm taking this bridge to Day Old Bakery Land.

TROLL

Oh, yeah? Well, this is a troll bridge, and if you want to cross, you're going to have to pay the troll.

LITTLE BILLY GOAT

But I don't have any money.

TROLL

Well then I guess I'm just going to have to eat you, because I'm a troll and that's what trolls do. We trolls have a saying: I like billy goats, especially for lunch. Billy goats are tasty, munch, munch, munch.

LITTLE BILLY GOAT

Well, we little billy goats have a saying too: Trolls are ugly, trolls do stink. Before you eat me you better stop and think.

BIG BILLY GOAT

Then my little brother remembered what I'd said about my taking care of him.

LITTLE BILLY GOAT

You don't want to eat me. My brother, who is much bigger and tastier than I am, will be along any minute. Eating me would be like filling up on salad.

TROLL

Like a nice big chicken Caesar salad?

LITTLE BILLY GOAT

No, more like a tiny little house salad.

TROLL

I guess you're right. Get out of here, kid. You're bothering me.

LITTLE BILLY GOAT

Yeah!
(HE exits.)

TROLL

Kids these days.

BIG BILLY GOAT

So my littlest brother clip-clopped his way to Day Old Bakery Land. Soon my other brother and I were getting hungry, so we played rock, paper, scissors, to decide who should go next. But when you have hooves, like we do, it's always rock. Being the generous brother that I am, I decided to let him go next. He was going across the bridge wearing tap shoes, so he went trip-trop, trip-trop, trip-trop, when who should appear, but big-nose himself.

TROLL

What are you doing on my bridge?

MIDDLE BILLY GOAT

Shuffle ball change.

TROLL

Well, speaking of change, this is a troll bridge, and if you want to cross, you're going to have to pay the troll.

MIDDLE BILLY GOAT

But I don't have any money.

TROLL

Then I'm going to eat you because I'm a troll and that's what trolls do. We have a saying: I like billy goats, especially for lunch. Billy goats are tasty, munch, munch, munch.

MIDDLE BILLY GOAT

Well, we middle billy goats have a saying too: Trolls are ugly, trolls do stink. Trolls look really bad in pink. Besides, you don't want to eat me. That would be like filling up on appetizers.

TROLL

Like a big plate of garlic bread?

MIDDLE BILLY GOAT

No, more like a light broth. You want my brother. He's a much larger portion than I am.

TROLL

You wouldn't kid a troll, would you?

MIDDLE BILLY GOAT

No.

TROLL

All right.

MIDDLE BILLY GOAT

Yeah!
(HE exits.)

BIG BILLY GOAT

Well, I was starting to get really hungry, and a little worried because I hadn't heard from either of my brothers, so I started across the bridge. I was wearing sandals at the time, so I went flip-flop, flip-flop, flip-flop. Just as I was getting to the other side, guess who poked his pointy head up? Yep, it was that ugly old . . .

TROLL

Hey! Watch it with those wisecracks. I've been listening to you narrating, and you're not being very flattering. I'll have you know that for a troll, I'm gorgeous.

BIG BILLY GOAT

Whatever. Say, have you seen two little kids come by here?

TROLL

Yes I have. In fact, they mentioned you specifically. I let them go so I wouldn't ruin my appetite for you, Mr. Main Course. I'm going to eat you because I'm a troll and that's what trolls do. Perhaps you've heard our little saying: I like billy goats, especially for lunch. Billy goats are tasty, munch, munch, munch.

BIG BILLY GOAT

Well, we big billy goats have a saying, too: Trolls are ugly and trolls do stink. Now get out of my way before I take a real dislike to you and knock you off this bridge!

TROLL

No chance, goat!

BIG BILLY GOAT

Charge!

TROLL

I only take cash.
(THEY fight and BIG BILLY GOAT wins.)

BIG BILLY GOAT

So I joined my brothers in Day Old Bakery Land and we celebrated with a big party.

Curtain

Suggested Musicals for Young Actors

Here are some musicals that you may enjoy performing. The cast size indicates if the number of actors needed is small (under 10), medium (under 20), or large (more than 20). You may be able to get some of these scripts at the library, while others are available only through a publishing company. You need to get permission from the publishing company and pay royalties for all public performances of these plays. The Samuel French Publishing Company represents many of these plays. You may write to them at Samuel French Inc., 45 W. 25th Street, Dept. W, New York, NY 10010. Your library can help you find where to write for permission and royalty information for other scripts.

Annie

Cast size   Large

Characters and Setting   Scenes go back and forth from a poor orphanage filled with little girls to the mansion of a millionaire and his staff. Set in New York City.

Music   "Tomorrow" is the most famous song, along with the orphan song "It's a Hard Knock Life."

Babes in Toyland

Cast size   Large

Characters and Setting   Mother-Goose-type characters such as Little Bo Peep and Jack and Jill. Set in a magical land.

Music   "Toyland" is the most famous song.

Cinderella

Cast size   Medium

Characters and Setting   Traditional Cinderella characters. Set in a fairy-tale land.

Music   Rodgers and Hammerstein's famous lyrics and melodies.

Fiddler on the Roof

Cast size   Large

Characters and Setting   There are roles for all ages in this musical about Jewish culture, traditions, and the old way of life. Set in a village in Russia.

Music   Upbeat songs such as "Matchmaker" and "If I Were a Rich Man," as well as ballads like "Sunrise, Sunset."

Free to Be You and Me

Cast size   Medium

Characters and Setting   Various characters in stories about self-esteem and cooperation. Set varies in each scene.

Music 1970s upbeat songs.

Joseph and the Amazing Technicolor Dreamcoat

Cast size   Large

Characters and Setting   Although a predominantly male cast, female roles can be added (often three women play the narrator). The play is set in biblical times, but some characters are based on such modern celebrities as Elvis Presley.

Music   Rock and roll.

Oliver

Cast size   Large

Characters and Setting   Many young children play orphans and a group of young thieves. Despite some sad parts, a happy ending prevails. Set in late-1800s England.

Music   "Food, Glorious Food" is one of the upbeat songs, amidst many beautiful ballads.

Once Upon A Mattress

Cast size   Large

Characters and Setting   Story, characters, and setting based on the story of *The Princess and the Pea*.

Music   Renaissance-sounding songs such as "Normandy," as well as big musical theater numbers such as "Happily Ever After."

Peter Pan

Cast size   Large

Characters and Setting   There are fun roles of all sizes in this musical, including the pirates and the lost boys. Set in Neverland.

Music   "I Won't Grow Up," "I Gotta Crow," and "Uggawug" are just a few of the many upbeat songs.

Really Rosie

Cast size   Small

Characters and Setting   Characters are based on children's stories. Set in New York City.

Music   Carole King wrote the upbeat songs that teach as well as entertain.

School House Rock Live

Cast size   Small

Characters and Setting   A true ensemble play where all the characters work together to teach lessons about grammar, history, multiplication, and science in a fun way. Set in a school teacher's house on the first day of school.

Music   Folk and rock and roll of the 1970s.

The Sound of Music

Cast size   Large

Characters and Setting   The von Trapp family with children of various ages. Set in beautiful Austria.

Music   "Do-Re-Mi," "Edelweiss," "My Favorite Things," and of course the title song are favorites for people of all ages.

The Wizard of Oz

Cast size   Large

Characters and Setting   This play has many parts for all ages and sizes. Set in the wonderful land of Oz.

Music   The audience will be singing along to their favorite songs, such as "Somewhere Over the Rainbow."

You're a Good Man, Charlie Brown

Cast size   Small

Characters and Setting   Charles Schulz's comic-strip characters hop out of the funny pages and onto the stage. Set is the *Peanuts* characters' neighborhood.

Music   Mostly jazz, but Lucy does sing a song to the music of Schroeder's beloved Beethoven.

Summaries of Plays Mentioned in the Book

1776   A musical that tells the story of John Hancock, Benjamin Franklin, John Adams, and other historical figures during the summer of 1776. (Based on a concept by Sherman Edwards, book by Peter Stone, music and lyrics by Sherman Edwards.)

Alice in Wonderland   A book by Lewis Carroll that has been made into many different versions of plays and musicals. It follows a young girl, Alice, as she travels through a magical land and meets unusual characters such as the White Rabbit and the Queen of Hearts.

Annie   A musical based on the comic strip *Little Orphan Annie*. It tells the story of an orphan girl who wins the heart of a millionaire. (Book by Thomas Meehan, music by Charles Strouse, lyrics by Martin Charnin.)

Annie Get Your Gun   A musical based on the legend of the real-life heroine, Annie Oakley. (Book by Herbert and Dorothy Fields, music and lyrics by Irving Berlin.)

Babes in Toyland   A musical about Mother Goose characters in a magical land and their triumph over an evil villain. (Book and lyrics by Nick DiMartino, music by Victor Herbert.)

Beauty and the Beast   A fairy tale by the Brothers Grimm that has been made into a number of plays and musicals. The most famous version of this tale is by Disney, first as an animated feature and then as a Broadway musical.

Big River   A musical about Huckleberry Finn, who befriends a runaway slave. Together the two venture down the Mississippi River. (Based on the book *The Adventures of Huckleberry Finn* by Mark Twain, music by Roger Miller, libretto by William Hauptmann.)

Brigadoon   A musical telling the tale of two tourists who discover a mythical village that only appears every hundred years. (Music by Frederick Loewe, book and lyrics by Alan J. Lerner.)

Bye Bye Birdie   A musical about a teen idol being drafted and the nationwide frenzy that ensues. (Book by Mike Stewart, music by Charles Strouse, lyrics by Lee Adams.)

Camelot   A musical based on the story of King Arthur, the knights of the round table, and the loves of Queen Guenevere. (Based on the book *The Once and Future King* by T. H. White, book and lyrics by Alan J. Lerner, music by Frederick Loewe.)

Candide   A musical that follows the adventures of the character Candide, which include an earthquake, a robbery, a shipwreck, and lost love. (Book adapted from Voltaire by Hugh Wheeler, music by Leonard Bernstein, and lyrics by Richard Wilbur, with additional lyrics by Stephen Sondheim and John Latouche.)

Carousel   A musical about a ghost who is allowed to visit earth for one day to do a good deed. (Adapted from the play *Liliom* by Ferenc Molnar, music and lyrics by Richard Rodgers and Oscar Hammerstein.)

Cats   A musical that tells the stories of different cat characters through music, poetry, and dance. (Based on the book of poems *Old Possum's Book of Practical Cats* by T.S. Eliot, music and lyrics by Andrew Lloyd Webber.)

A Chorus Line   A musical that takes place at a dance audition. Each auditioner gets to tell his story through the course of the play. (Book by James Kirkwood and Nicholas Dante, music by Marvin Hamlisch, lyrics by Edward Kleban.)

Cinderella   A fairy tale written by the Brothers Grimm that has been made into numerous plays and musicals, most notably by Richard Rodgers and Oscar Hammerstein.

City of Angels   A musical set in Los Angeles about a movie genre called film noir (crime stories with villains, usually set in seedy places). (Music by Cy Coleman, lyrics by David Zippel.)

Crazy for You   An aspiring actor puts on a show in Nevada and falls in love with the theater owner's daughter. This is a newer version of the musical *Girl Crazy*. (Book by Ken Ludwig, music and lyrics by George and Ira Gershwin.)

Damn Yankees   A musical that tells the story of a man who sells his soul to the devil in exchange for becoming a baseball hero. (Based on the novel *The Year the Yankees Lost the Pennant* by Douglass Wallop, book by George Abbott and Douglass Wallop, music and lyrics by Richard Adler and Jerry Ross.)

A Doctor in Spite of Himself   A French farce by Molière. It tells the story of a man who pretends to be a doctor in order to gain wealth and respect.

Evita   A musical that tells the story of Eva Peron's rise to power in Argentina. (Music by Andrew Lloyd Webber, lyrics by Tim Rice.)

The Fantasticks A musical that tells the story of young love and life changes that people undergo as they grow and mature. (Book and lyrics by Tom Jones, music by Harvey Schmidt.)

Fiddler on the Roof A musical about Jewish traditions as it follows the story of Tevye and his family through marriages and hardships. (Based on stories by Sholem Aleichem, book by Joseph Stein, music by Jerry Bock, lyrics by Sheldon Harnick.)

Finian's Rainbow A musical about an Irishman and his daughter who journey to the mythical town of Rainbow Valley. Based on a Celtic fairy tale, this story includes a goblin character named Og. (Book by E. Y. Harburg and Fred Saidy, music by Burton Lane, lyrics by E. Y. Harburg.)

Follie A musical that tells the story of the closing of Dimitri Weissman's theater and his final show. (Book by James Goldman, music by Stephen Sondheim.)

Funny Girl A musical revue by Jule Styne about Fanny Brice, a comedienne who made it big in Zeigfeld's Follies. (Book by Isobel Lennart, music by Jule Styne, lyrics by Bob Merrill.)

A Funny Thing Happened on the Way to the Forum A musical that follows the crazy tale of a Roman slave who is trying to gain his freedom. (Book by Burt Shevelove and Larry Gelbart, music and lyrics by Stephen Sondheim.)

Girl Crazy The original version of the musical *Crazy for You.* (Book by Ken Ludwig, music and lyrics by George and Ira Gershwin.)

Grease A musical featuring rock and roll, this is a love story set in a high school in the 1950s. (Book, music, and lyrics by Jim Jacobs and Warren Casey.)

Hansel and Gretal A fairy tale by the Brothers Grimm that has been made into a number of plays, including an opera.

Hello Dolly This musical tells the story of Dolly Levi, a matchmaker, and her efforts to match up couples, including herself and the wealthy Horace Vandergelder. (Based on the play *The Matchmaker* by Thornton Wilder, written by Jerry Herman.)

How to Succeed in Business Without Really Trying A musical that follows the character J. Pierpont Finch as he climbs the ladder of the corporate world. (Based on the novel by Shepherd Mead, book by Abe Burrows, Jack Weinstock, and Willie Gilbert, music and lyrics by Frank Loesser.)

Into the Woods A musical that combines a number of Grimm fairy tales and explores what happens after "happily ever after." (Book by James Lapine, music and lyrics by Stephen Sondheim.)

Jack and the Beanstalk   A fairy tale that tells the story of Jack, who is sent to the market by his mother to sell their cow and comes back with magic beans. The story of Jack and the Beanstalk is included in *Into the Woods*.

Jesus Christ Superstar   A musical that tells the story of Jesus Christ using rock and roll music. (Music by Andrew Lloyd Webber, lyrics by Tim Rice.)

Joseph and the Amazing Technicolor Dreamcoat   A musical that follows the biblical story of Joseph from his father Joseph's home to his success in Egypt. (Music by Andrew Lloyd Webber, lyrics by Tim Rice.)

Jungle Book   Rudyard Kipling's collection of stories about Mowgli, an Indian boy raised by wolves. There are a number of play versions of this story as well as a Disney animated feature film.

The King and I   A musical based on the diaries of Anna Harriette. It tells of her experiences as a nanny for King Mongkut, the King of Siam. (Book and lyrics by Oscar Hammerstein, music by Richard Rodgers.)

Kiss Me Kate   A musical that features a play within a play. The characters are actors performing in *The Taming of the Shrew*; their roles parallel their own lives. (Based on *The Taming of the Shrew* by William Shakespeare, book by Bella and Sam Spewack, music and lyrics by Cole Porter.)

Les Misérables (called "*Les Mis*" for short)   A musical that tells a story of power, pride, and love during the French Revolution. (Based on the novel by Victor Hugo, adapted by Alain Boublil and Claude-Michel Schonberg, music by Claude-Michel Schonberg, lyrics by Herbert Kretzmer.)

The Little Mermaid   A fairy tale about a mermaid who wants to become a human being. There are several play versions of this fairy tale by the Brothers Grimm as well as a Disney animated musical feature.

Little Shop of Horrors   A comedy about a people-eating plant and the man who tries to stop it. (Based on the film by Roger Corman, book and lyrics by Howard Ashman, music by Alan Menken.)

A Midsummer Night's Dream   A comedy by William Shakespeare. Set in ancient times, it includes fairies and complicated love stories to add to its charm.

Miss Saigon   A musical about a love story that takes place in Saigon during the Vietnam War. (Book by Alain Boublil and Claude-Michel Schonberg, music by Claude-Michel Schonberg, lyrics by Richard Maltby, Jr., and Alain Boublil.)

The Music Man   A musical about a con man who falls for a small-town librarian. (Based on a story by Meredith Wilson and Franklin Lacey, book, music, and lyrics by Meredith Wilson.)

My Fair Lady   A musical that tells the story of Eliza Doolittle and Professor Henry Higgins, who tries to turn Eliza into a proper lady. (Based on the play *Pygmalion* by George Bernard Shaw, book and lyrics by Alan J. Lerner, music by Frederick Loewe.)

No, No, Nanette   A musical that takes place at a vacation cottage near Atlantic City. It is about the host's comical, embarrassing secrets and what happens when they come out. (Book by Otto Harbach and Frank Mandel, music by Vincent Youmans, lyrics by Irving Caesar.)

Oklahoma   A musical about pretty young Laurey who must choose between two men in the midst of cowboys and farmers. (Book, music, and lyrics by Richard Rodgers and Oscar Hammerstein.)

Oliver   A story of an orphan boy who gets mixed up with crooks and pickpockets before finding his relatives. (Based on the book *Oliver Twist* by Charles Dickens, book, music, and lyrics by Oliver Bart.)

Once Upon a Mattress   A musical that tells the tale of a princess who must pass a test of sensitivity in order to marry the prince. (Based on the Grimm fairy tale *The Princess and the Pea*, book by Jay Thompson, Dean Fuller, and Marshall Barer, music by Mary Rodgers, lyrics by Marshall Barer.)

Our Town   The story of life in a New Hampshire town; the play follows its characters through love, happiness, and sorrow. (By Thornton Wilder.)

Peter Pan   A story about a boy and his adventures in Neverland, where he will never have to grow up. There are a number of plays and musicals based on this story, including a Disney animated feature. (Based on a book by James M. Barrie.)

Phantom   A musical about a deformed phantom who lives under an opera house. (Based on the book *The Phantom of the Opera* by Gaston Leroux, book by Arthur Kopit, music and lyrics by Maury Yeston.)

The Pirates of Penzance   Love, life, and humor with pirates, police officers, and a wacky major general. (An operetta by Gilbert and Sullivan.)

Really Rosie   A musical about a day in the life of Rosie, a creative child who makes all of her friends star in a make-believe movie with her. (Book and lyrics by Maurice Sendak, music by Carole King.)

Rent   A rock and roll version of Puccini's opera *La Boheme*. (By Jonathan Larson.)

Robin Hood   A legendary tale about a man who led a band of outlaws in Sherwood Forest in order to steal from the rich and give to the poor. A story from English folklore that has been made into numerous books, plays, and movies.

Romeo and Juliet   Two lovers risk everything to be together even though their families have forbidden them to do so. (By William Shakespeare.)

School House Rock Live   A musical that teaches the parts of speech, multiplication, history, and science through songs. This play is based on the short, animated *School House Rock* television programs. (Adapted by Theatre BAM, music by Lynn Ahrens, Bob Dorough, and Dave Frishberg.)

Show Boat   A musical set on a paddle-wheel riverboat, it is about show business and interracial marriage. (Based on a novel by Edna Ferber, music and lyrics by Jerome Kern and Oscar Hammerstein.)

Singing in the Rain   A musical that tells the story of how movies went from silent films to "talkies." (Based on the MGM film of the same name, screenplay and adaptation by Betty Comden and Adolph Green, songs by Nacio Herb Brown and Arthur Freed.)

The Sound of Music   A musical set during World War II about a nun-turned-governess, Maria, who falls in love with the widowed father Baron von Trapp. Together with the children they create a singing troupe, which helps them flee the Nazis. (Music and lyrics by Richard Rodgers and Oscar Hammerstein.)

South Pacific   A love story that deals with prejudice during wartime. (Music and lyrics by Richard Rodgers and Oscar Hammerstein.)

Starlight Express   A *Little Engine That Could* story about a boy's trains coming to life. Performed on roller skates, this is a musical set against the background of a steel bridge. (Music and lyrics by Andrew Lloyd Webber.)

Sweeny Todd   A scary tale about a demon barber and his evil plans. (Based on a version of *Sweeny Todd* by Christopher Bond, book by Hugh Wheeler, music and lyrics by Stephen Sondheim.)

The Tale of Peter Rabbit   A story about a rabbit who sneaks into Mr. MacGreggor's garden and gets into all kinds of trouble. This book by Beatrix Potter has been adapted into a number of play versions.

Taming of the Shrew   A play about a fiery young woman and the man who attempts to tame her. (By William Shakespeare.)

Titanic   A musical version of the sinking of the *Titanic* and the people who were aboard that fateful cruise. (Music and lyrics by Maury Yeston, book by Margot McGraw.)

Tommy   A rock and roll musical about a boy who can't hear, speak, or see, but who manages to become a pinball champion. (By the rock group *The Who*.)

West Side Story   A musical that resets the story of *Romeo and Juliet* in New York City and tells a story of rival gangs rather than feuding families. (Based on a concept by Jerome Robbins, book by Arthur Laurents, music by Leonard Bernstein, lyrics by Stephen Sondheim.)

The Wiz   This is a rock and roll, gospel, and disco musical that retells the classic story of *The Wizard of Oz*. (Based on the book *The Wonderful Wizard of Oz* by L. Frank Baum, book by William F. Brown, music and lyrics by Charlie Smalls.)

The Wonderful Wizard of Oz   A book by L. Frank Baum that was adapted for a movie musical version and numerous play versions. The story of a young girl who travels to the magical land of Oz, where she has many adventures and discovers that there's no place like home.

Working   A musical where many different people tell stories about what it's like to do their job. (Based on the book *Working* by Studs Terkel, adapted by Stephen Schwartz and Nina Faso, with songs by Craig Carnelia, Micki Grant, Mary Rodgers, Susan Birkenhead, Stephen Schwartz, and James Taylor.)

You're a Good Man, Charlie Brown   A musical based on the comic strip *Peanuts* by Charles Schulz. Short scenes and songs show the lives of Charlie Brown, Snoopy, Lucy, Linus, Schroeder, and Peppermint Patty.

Bibliography

Blum, Bessie, editor. *Musicals: An Illustrated Historical Overview*. New York: Barron's Educational Series Inc., 1988.

Edom, Helen and Nicola Katrak. *Starting Ballet*. Tulsa, Oklahoma: Usborne First Skills, EDC Publishing, 1992.

Gottfried, Martin. *Broadway Musicals*. The Netherlands: Harry N. Abrams B.V., 1979.

Music Theatre International. *Music Theatre International Catalog*. New York: Music Theatre International, 1988.

Samuel French, Inc. *1998 Supplement to Basic Catalogue of Plays and Musicals*. New York: Samuel French, Inc., 1998.

Samuel French, Inc. *Musicals from the House of Plays*. New York: Samuel French, Inc.,1998.

Willis, John, editor. *Theatre World*, 1981-1982 Season, Volume 38. New York: Crown Publishers Inc., 1983.

About the Author

Lisa Bany-Winters began performing in community musicals at the age of 11. She founded the Emanon Theater Company and began directing children's productions when she was 15 years old. Emanon is now an established professional theater company with a talented ensemble of actors who, under Lisa's direction, create original adaptations of children's classics through improvisation. Emanon has performed regularly at the Halsted Theatre Centre, the Body Politic Theatre, the Second City Northwest, and has toured to schools, festivals, camps, and libraries throughout the Chicago area.

She comes from a musical family with a jazz musician for a father. He played for a musical review called *Compliments of Cole* when Lisa was a child. She attended the play every Sunday and memorized dozens of Cole Porter songs. Later she worked for the National Jewish Theater, where they created musical reviews of Jewish Tin Pan Alley song-

writers, including Irving Berlin, George Gershwin, Richard Rodgers, and Harold Arlen.

Lisa is currently the kids director for Northlight Theater located at the North Shore Center for the Performing Arts in Skokie, Illinois. She teaches acting and improvisation and directs kids' theater and Theater Camp at the Center.

Lisa has taught improvisation and creative drama at the Second City Northwest and to students from Cabrini Green, a Chicago public housing development.

Lisa is the author of *On Stage: Theater Games and Activities for Kids*, and the plays section of the *Children's Book of Knowledge*.

A graduate of Columbia College, Lisa lives with her husband, Brian Winters, and her daughter, Michaela in Glenview, Illinois. She is a champion at the game "Who Wrote This Song?"

Photo: Glenn Herr

Lisa Bany-Winters with her daughter Michaela "Tinkerbell" Bany-Winters.

More Books by Lisa Bany-Winters from Chicago Review Press

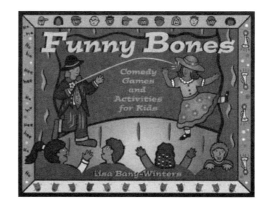

On Stage
Theater Games and Activities for Kids

• Parents' Choice Approved Seal

"Bany-Winters . . . has compiled a varied and interesting assortment of theater games that will stimulate the imagination and get young thespians ready to perform on stage."

—*Booklist*

"A useful resource for ensemble-building games for student-run drama groups and rehearsal techniques for adult teachers/directors. . . . A terrific addition to drama collections. Purchase an extra copy for the professional shelf as well."

—*School Library Journal*

Funny Bones
Comedy Games and Activities for Kids

• A Smithsonian Notable Book for Children

"A clever compendium of exercises and scripts."
—*Smithsonian*

"Chock full of comedic activities. . . . Ideal for birthday parties and budding comedians."
—*Children's Bookwatch*

**Both books are available at your local bookstore
or by calling (800)-888-4741**

CHICAGO REVIEW PRESS

www.chicagoreviewpress.com

**Distributed by Independent Publishers Group
www.ipgbook.com**